Herbert Read

# ALL THAT WAS LEFT OF THEM

writings on war

Edited by Benedict Read
Introduced by James Read

with illustrations from the first world war
by Herbert Read

The **Orage** Press
2014

This book is published by The **Orage** Press
16A Heaton Road
Mitcham
Surrey CR4 2BU
England

Herbert Read's writings and images: © 2014 Herbert Read Trust
Preface: © 2014 Benedict Read
Introduction: © 2014 James Read

All rights are reserved under English, European Union and international law. No part of this publication may be reproduced, stored in a retrieval system or transmitted in any form or by any means, electronic, mechanical, photocopying, recording or otherwise, without prior permission in writing of the copyright holders.

ISBN: 978-0-9929247-1-3

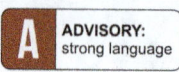

Herbert Read

# ALL THAT WAS LEFT OF THEM

**Benedict Read** is Herbert Read's youngest son, and a distinguished art historian in his own right. As well as being the world's leading authority on nineteenth-century British sculpture, he has written extensively on Victorian architecture and on twentieth century sculpture, including the ground-breaking study on inter-war British sculpture, entitled *Sculpture in Britain Between the Wars*. He is a Fellow of the Society of Antiquaries and has worked at the Courtauld Institute of Art (University of London) and the University of Leeds, where he now holds the title of Senior Visiting Research Fellow in Fine Art.

**James Read** is one of Herbert Read's grandsons. Having followed in his Grandfather's footsteps by studying at the University of Leeds, he is now a journalist with the BBC World Service.

# CONTENTS

| | |
|---|---|
| PREFACE BY BENEDICT READ | 11 |
| INTRODUCTION BY JAMES READ | 14 |

*FIRST WORLD WAR POEMS (1914-1918)*

| | |
|---|---|
| AEROPLANES | 35 |
| YPRES | 38 |
| THE AUTUMN OF THE WORLD | 41 |
| CHAMP DE MANOEUVRES | 42 |
| MOVEMENT OF TROOPS | 44 |
| NAKED WARRIORS | 46 |
| PARODY OF A FORGOTTEN BEAUTY | 47 |
| KNEESHAW GOES TO WAR | 48 |
| THE SCENE OF WAR | |
|     I. VILLAGES DÉMOLIS | 57 |
|     II. THE CRUCIFIX | 58 |
|     III. FEAR | 59 |
|     IV. THE HAPPY WARRIOR | 60 |
|     V. LIEDHOLZ | 61 |
|     VI. THE REFUGEES | 62 |
|     VII. MY COMPANY | 63 |
|     VIII. THE EXECUTION OF CORNELIUS VANE | 68 |
| AUGURIES OF LIFE AND DEATH | 74 |

*FROM THE CONTRARY EXPERIENCE: AUTOBIOGRAPHIES*

| | |
|---|---|
| THE IMPACT OF WAR | 80 |
| INTRODUCTION TO A WAR DIARY | 95 |
| EXTRACTS FROM A WAR DIARY | 100 |
| THE RAID | 144 |
| IN RETREAT | 154 |

*REVIEWS WRITTEN BETWEEN THE WARS*

| | |
|---|---|
| A LOST GENERATION | 193 |
| MORE WAR BOOKS I | 198 |
| MORE WAR BOOKS II | 203 |
| HISTORY AND REALITY | 207 |
| THE FAILURE OF THE WAR BOOKS | 212 |

*FROM THE END OF WAR (1933)*

| | |
|---|---|
| MEDITATION OF A DYING GERMAN OFFICER | 220 |
| DIALOGUE BETWEEN THE BODY AND THE SOUL OF THE MURDERED GIRL | 226 |
| MEDITATION OF THE WAKING ENGLISH OFFICER | 232 |

*WRITINGS ON THE SPANISH CIVIL WAR*

| | |
|---|---|
| BOMBING CASUALTIES IN SPAIN | 240 |
| THE HEART CONSCRIPTED | 241 |
| LAMENT FOR SPAIN | 242 |
| NEARER TO REALITY | 244 |
| THE PRE-REQUISITE OF PEACE | 247 |

*SECOND WORLD WAR POEMS (1939-1945)*

| | |
|---|---|
| LOGOS | 252 |
| TO A CONSCRIPT OF 1940 | 253 |
| ODE (*Written during the Battle of Dunkirk, May, 1940*) | 255 |
| WAR AND PEACE | 265 |
| THE CONTRARY EXPERIENCE | 266 |
| A WORLD WITHIN A WAR | 269 |
| A SHORT POEM FOR ARMISTICE DAY | 278 |
| 1945 | 280 |

## "FREEDOM IS IT A CRIME?"
## POST-WAR WRITINGS ON ANARCHISM AND PACIFISM

| | |
|---|---|
| BEFORE THE TRIAL | 282 |
| AFTER THE TRIAL | 287 |
| AMNESTY CAMPAIGN | 294 |
| THE PROBLEM OF WAR AND PEACE | 297 |
| A ONE-MAN MANIFESTO | 304 |
| DISOBEDIENCE | 311 |
| DECLARATION | 314 |

*Image: photograph from 1 April 1918 of the surviving officers of Herbert Read's battalion following the Second Battle of the Somme, 21 to 28 March 1918.*

*Page 10: Read's notes on the survivors on the back of the photograph.*

CARTE POSTALE

Correspondance  Adresse

ALL THAT WAS LEFT OF THEM.
2nd Battle of the Somme. March 21-28. 1918.

Back Row. (left to right). Simpson – Stockeld – the Padre – Colin – Howard – Bingham – Hall.

Middle Row:– Pickard (Q.M.) – Lund (C.O.) – "ME" – The Doc (WHITE).

Bottom Row:– Roxby – "Nannie" – Hibbert.

Taken April 1. 1918.

# PREFACE
## BENEDICT READ

This volume brings together my father's War Writings in poetry and prose. Many have been republished since their first appearance, starting with *Naked Warriors* in 1919. But my father was bibliographically complex. He would publish poems sometimes in journals in isolation as well as in the various editions of *Collected Poems* of 1926, 1946, 1953 and 1966. In these latter he would exclude some previously featured and add others. The major prose writings such as *In Retreat* have been republished over the years but the book reviews covering War and the politics of War have not been seen since their original journal appearances in the 1920s and 1930s, though the articles to do with war and anarchism were republished by David Goodway and Freedom Press in *A One-Man Manifesto* of 1994 - their original appearances are duly cited.

These though in their immediacy add an additional element to the life-long effect of my father's war experiences between 1914 and 1919. Over his entire lifetime as a writer he returned in such differing contexts to the impact of the undoubtedly traumatic experience of World War I and this is what is reflected in the present volume. In addition it is illustrated by the largely unpublished drawings and watercolours he himself executed in the war period.

I am very grateful to my nephew James Read for his well researched examination of my father's war experience. I am grateful to the staff of Special Collections, the Brotherton Library, University of Leeds for their help in retrieving some of the rarer material previously not republished, to Layla Bloom, Curator of the Audrey and Stanley Burton Gallery at Leeds University for extra assistance with this, and to Leeds University's Digitising team for preparing the illustrative material. Dr Michael Paraskos has as ever been invaluable in preparing the material for publication, as has Angela Witney for secretarial assistance.

The photograph of the grave of my Uncle Charles, killed in action in 1918, was taken by myself when on pilgrimage to his grave with my nephew and with my cousin Charles and his grandchildren in July 2014. I am very grateful for their interest and encouragement.

Benedict Read FSA<br>Leeds, September 2014

# INTRODUCTION
## JAMES READ

*All the world is wet with tears
and droops its languid life
in sympathy.
But death is beautiful with pride: the trees
are golden lances whose brave array
assails the sadness of the day.*

- from *Auguries of Life and Death*
by Herbert Read

Herbert Read was one of the most prominent British intellectuals of the mid-twentieth century. Best known as a champion of modern art, he was also a literary critic and publisher, an educationalist and cultural theorist, and an outspoken advocate of anarchism. He wrote more than sixty books, the most influential of which included *Education through Art* and *Art and Society*. But before all that, he was a poet and a soldier in the First World War.

Herbert Read was also my grandfather, though he died the year before I was born. As a boy I spent many holidays at Stonegrave, the rural home where he lived for his last two decades after returning to his native North Yorkshire. The house was full of paintings and sculptures by the artists he had championed, from Henry Moore and Barbara Hepworth to Rene Magritte and Joan Miro. The shelves were lined with his own books translated into many languages, as well hundreds of others he published or reviewed. But one artefact fascinated me above all. In a drawer in his study was a sleek black automatic pistol in a leather holster, in full working order and complete with spare magazine (though fortunately, given my youthful enthusiasm, no ammunition). My grandfather had taken it as a souvenir from a German officer he captured in 1916 in no-man's land, during a night raid on the enemy trenches.

Read fought for the best part of three years as infantry officer on the Western Front, rising to the rank of Captain and being awarded the MC and the DSO for bravery. The experience transformed and defined him, just as it transformed everyone who took part and defined the world that followed. It left him a committed pacifist and anarchist, convinced that war was the ultimate evil and the state was to blame. But at the same time he took pride in his ability to endure the horror and lead men into battle, and looked back on the intense comradeship and unanimity of combat as 'days of danger and of joy shared together' Even though the struggle had been futile, he believed the solidarity and self-sacrifice shown by the men who fought was nonetheless glorious, and it left him with an enduring faith in humanity. This contradiction – which he described as 'the paradox of hope in the midst of despair' – sets him apart from other more celebrated war poets, and is much harder to comprehend than the simple narrative of pointless slaughter in the mud.

The First World War is almost universally remembered as a terrible loss of innocence. Read had already had one personal idyll shattered. He was born in 1893 at Muscoates Grange in North Yorkshire as the eldest son of a tenant farmer. But when his father died suddenly in 1902 the family lost the tenancy and Herbert, aged nine, was sent to an orphanage school in Halifax. On leaving school he joined his mother, who had taken work in Leeds, and thanks to a loan from an uncle he was able to enrol at the university, where he was exposed to modernist ideas and radical politics. But a romanticism inspired by his childhood on the farm never left him. He always looked back on it as an Arcadian existence, beautifully evoked in his book *The Innocent Eye*. Together with the war, he saw it as the key formative experience of his life and the journey from agrarian idyll to the horror of the trenches – from innocence to experience – lay at the heart of his character.

Read was still a student when the war broke out in August 1914, and as a member of the university Officer Training Corps he was already in uniform. Even then he considered himself a socialist and pacifist, but these convictions were not fully formed. He later wrote that he viewed the outbreak of war as a disastrous clash between rival imperial powers that would be brought to an end by international working class action. But at the same time – like millions of young men across Europe – he was swept up by the excitement of the moment. Influenced by Nietzsche, Read saw war as a supreme test of manhood and character, a challenge he couldn't ignore. He volunteered without hesitation. His brothers, Billy and Charlie, did the same – though Charlie, aged seventeen, had to wait until he was old enough to fight. All around them thousands of men were volunteering each day. Britain hadn't fought a war in Europe for a century, and none of them knew what was coming.

In January 1915 Read was commissioned as an officer in the Yorkshire Regiment (The Green Howards) and sent to a training camp in Dorset. He was 21 and had never left his native county before. He was also newly orphaned – his mother Eliza had died the previous December. His initial experience of the army was disheartening. Almost all the other officers were from public schools – many from Eton. He was made to feel his social inferiority, and mocked in the mess for his modernist reading habits. He was equally cut-off from the rank-and-file, most of whom were miners. Yet this disunity did not last once they left England. Read quickly found that individual character rather than social superiority was what counted in battle, and that class differences meant little among men facing common danger.

Any romantic illusions Read had about war disappeared as soon as he joined his battalion at the front in Belgium in November 1915. The 7th Green Howards were in the Ypres Salient, where Britain's small regular army had been all but destroyed in the fighting of 1914. There was nothing there, he later wrote, but 'primitive filth, boredom, lice and death'. The British position was under fire from three sides by the Germans, who held the higher ground. The battlefield was a quagmire of mud littered with thousands of rotting corpses that made digging trenches difficult. Spells in the front line were followed by periods in reserve, sleeping in the ramparts and cellars of Ypres by day and carrying supplies forward under fire by night. There were constant casualties from snipers and shelling. Though not an immediate certainty, death was 'a probability a hundred times enacted'. Even the rest camp behind the lines was fetid with mud.

The war did not stop Read from embarking on a literary career. A fast and efficient post service kept him supplied with books that filled the long periods of boredom between action and provided his main escape from the horrors of the trenches. Even by the standards of the time, the range and variety of his reading was extraordinary. He kept in touch with the modernist circle he had encountered at the Leeds Arts Club. Throughout the war he was writing essays for the cultural journal *The New Age* and also helped found another, *Art and Letters*. His main correspondence was with Evelyn Roff, a fellow student he had met at university who would become his first wife after the war. His letters to her were published as a war diary in 1963, with the contents heavily edited to remove anything intimate and the originals burned. What remains provides a vital insight into how he felt about the war at the time. But above all the letters are filled with intellectual discussion of books and literary theory - at one point he half apologises for his obsession.

In an early sign of his vocation for art, Read carried a sketchbook into the trenches. And of course he was also writing poetry, seen in those days as a normal response to dramatic events. He had his first volume of poems, *Songs of Chaos*, published at his own expense before he crossed the Channel, but soon came to view these as embarrassingly naïve and had the remaining copies pulped. The war gave him something much more real to write about. His first war poems were published in 1916 in the Leeds University magazine *The Gryphon*. A full volume, *Naked Warriors,* came out in 1919. His aim as a poet, he said, was to tell the truth about what was happening in the hope that this could help bring the madness to an end. But poems changed nothing – not his or anyone else's - except how future generations would remember the war.

Read drew a growing self-confidence from his ability to cope with the appalling conditions of trench warfare in winter. But that endurance had its limits. On 31st March 1915 he was wounded and sent back to England to recover. His wound was relatively minor – a burn on his hand caused accidentally by a flare gun. The psychological damage suffered by his young mind was much greater. Army medical records reveal that he was treated for what the doctors called neurasthenia – a term encompassing nervous exhaustion as well as depression. In modern terminology, it seems clear he suffered a breakdown as a result of post-traumatic stress. Herbert never wrote about this. But his condition was far from unique. Trench warfare produced an epidemic of psychological casualties. Initially medical experts thought what they were dealing with was a physical condition caused by exposure to high explosive bombardment and called it shell shock – a name that stuck. But by 1915 they were coming to understand it as war neurosis - a psychological disorder caused by the prolonged strain of modern industrial warfare.

Each month he was in England, Read had to attend an army medical board to determine whether he was fit to return to battle. The army was beginning to recognise a grey area between cowardice and outright madness, and officers were treated far more sympathetically than the men. But the stigma attached to war neurosis was still great. More than three hundred British soldiers were executed for cowardice during the war – many of them were no doubt suffering from psychological breakdown. Read was acutely aware of this. Two of his best war poems tackle the boundary between fear and insanity, and the limit of individual endurance. The protagonist in 'Kneeshaw Goes to War' loses his nerve when his pick cleaves the skull of a corpse and is saved from his cowardice only by the 'merciful' explosion that sends him home minus a leg. 'The Execution of Cornelius Vane' is an even more sympathetic portrait of a soldier who cannot cope. Cornelius shoots off his trigger finger to escape combat, but is forced back into battle when the Germans break the line. Exposed to bombardment, he panics and flees, only to be arrested and executed.

But Kneeshaw and Vane are not portrayed simply as cowards. Above all they are individuals caught up in vast and terrible events that are completely beyond their control - 'a cog in some evil engine' or 'a fly in the sticky web of life'. This image of powerlessness recurs throughout Read's poetry – he felt himself swept up in a storm that was in some way beyond politics and certainly beyond his power to resist. Cornelius Vane's personal lament as he faces the firing squad is at once the cry of an entire generation sacrificed to war:

> What wrong have I done that I should leave these:
> The bright sun rising
> And the birds that sing?

Despite his professed pacifism, Read never seriously considered refusing to fight on political or moral grounds. Those who did faced extreme sanctions once conscription was introduced. While he was back in England a group of conscientious objectors who refused to serve in any capacity were imprisoned at Richmond Castle - the headquarters of the Green Howards. The Richmond 16 - as they were known - were taken out to France and sentenced to death, only to have their sentences commuted at the last moment. Read never mention this, but he must have been aware of it.

Unlike the war poets Wilfred Owen and Siegfried Sassoon, there is no evidence that Read was treated by a psychiatrist. After some time in hospital in London he was sent to Rugeley army camp in Staffordshire to recuperate. While he was there, Britain launched its biggest offensive of the war so far - the Battle of the Somme. On the first day alone almost 20,000 men were killed in the worst disaster in British military history. Read's battalion was one of those that went over the top into a storm of German machine-gun fire on 1st July 1916. In just three minutes more than 300 officers and men of the 7th Green Howards were killed or wounded attacking the village of Fricourt. By the time the battalion was withdrawn from the fighting ten days later, it had lost more than half its strength. Read doesn't mention this either, but he must also have known of it, and the slaughter of all those men he had fought alongside surely preyed on his mind. One of his finest poems, 'My Company', is an anguished lament for lost comrades. 'Oh beautiful men, Oh men I loved/Oh whither are you gone, my company?' The poem was written later in the war and may not have been about that specific unit. For Read was to lose other companies. In October 1916 he was passed fit to return to battle and in April 1917 he was sent back to France.

    Despite his growing political opposition to the war, Read went back to the fighting for the second time as a willing participant. Like many soldiers, he had found being in England an alienating experience after the comradeship and shared dangers of the trenches. 'I really feel extraordinarily calm and happy,' he wrote to Evelyn as he waited to go up to the line. He didn't hate the Germans or 'glory in fighting for fighting's sake', he said. But the desire to test himself – 'to leap into the clean sea of danger and self-sacrifice' - still burned strong. 'I don't want to die for king and country,' he asserts. 'If I do die it is for the salvation of my own soul'. Bravado aside, he may also have felt that he still had to prove himself and atone for missing the Somme, where so many of his men had been killed.

    By this time his brothers, Billy and Charlie, were also at the front. All three Read boys were involved in the great offensives of 1917, as Britain's 'New Armies' of citizen soldiers resumed their effort to break the German hold on Belgium and northern France. Herbert arrived as the first battle – Arras – was raging. He was assigned as a replacement to a different battalion, the 10th Green Howards, which had suffered heavy losses in the initial assault. He endured terrible days and nights in an isolated outpost under continuous bombardment as men were killed and maimed all around him. Even after this, his commitment to taking part, though not to the cause, remained strong. Writing a few weeks later, he admonished Evelyn for not understanding why he was there. 'If I were free today, I'm almost sure I would be compelled by every impulse within me to join this adventure,' he tells her, before promising to 'fight for socialism when the time comes'.

His youngest brother Charlie was next into battle. At 17 he had been too young to join up when war broke out but volunteered as soon as he was able. Initially a private, he was selected for officer training despite the youthful looks that earned him the nickname 'Baby'. Read had hoped he might join his battalion but he was given a commission in the 9th Green Howards. Charlie went into the attack on 7th June at the Battle of Messines, moments after the German defences along a ridge overlooking the Ypres Salient had been obliterated by huge mines buried deep underground. This was the biggest man-made explosion the world had ever seen and the assault was judged a success. But Charlie's battalion ran into a crossfire from the German reserve positions and he was hit in the leg by a machine-gun bullet. With characteristic cheerfulness, he wrote home that he had been 'lucky enough to get a blighty' – a wound just bad enough to be sent back to England.

Meanwhile, Billy was in the Ypres Salient preparing for the biggest British offensive of the year – the battle that became known as Passchendaele. He was a Lieutenant in 12th Battalion King's Own Yorkshire Light Infantry – a unit of miners and pioneers that was engaged in building roads and railways through the Flanders mud as well as manning the trenches. In the early hours of 31st July – just before the attack – he was hit by a German shell. His wounds to the left thigh and buttock put him out of the war. After many months in hospital Billy was able to walk again, but his disability meant he could never realise his dream of returning to the land as a farmer like his father. His award of the Military Cross for bravery and devotion to duty was scant consolation.

If Read was looking for a chance to prove himself, he did not have to wait long. The very same night Billy was wounded, he was back in action near Arras, leading a night raid on the German trenches to capture a prisoner. Such raids were seen by the generals as a good way of fostering fighting spirit and dominating no-man's land, as well as a source of intelligence. The troops generally viewed them as dangerous stunts that risked heavy casualties for little real gain. Read's raid was a key moment in his personal war. Writing to Evelyn shortly before, he describes it as a 'death or glory job' and says he is glad of a chance to show his fellow soldiers he is 'of the clan that don't care a damn for anything'. In the event, it went well. As they crept by night across no-man's land, he and his men encountered a German patrol out repairing the barbed wire. At the critical moment, Read's nerve held. He fired first (the only time, he later said, he deliberately tried to kill a man rather than shooting at masses of advancing troops) and captured a German officer. The objective was achieved without having to enter the German trenches and his men were able to withdraw before the inevitable retaliatory shelling. In the poem 'Liedholz', the name of his prisoner, he plays the incident for irony and suggests a meeting of minds: 'In broken French we discussed/Beethoven, Nietzsche and the International'. His prose account 'The Raid', published in 1930, is altogether darker. His men are 'lusting to kill' the prisoner and his Colonel, a drunken coward, demands they cut off his finger so he can take his signet-ring. Liedholz found Read's blackened face terrifying rather than amusing, and was less interested in discussing Nietzsche than in 'passionately defending the German cause' in terms of racial superiority.

For leading the raid, Read was awarded the Military Cross for bravery. He had proved himself in the eyes of his battalion and 'The Raid' is above all a meditation on the mechanics of fear, a constant theme in his war poetry. He admits being afraid as he crept towards the enemy lines in the dark. But once action is joined, he is 'suddenly calm' and 'filled with a great exaltation'. His conclusion is that fear is an inevitable physical reaction to danger, 'a sudden jet of pus into the bloodstream', that only 'men of imagination' such as himself can overcome. The officer named only as P, who refuses to lead the raid, is probably a fictional alter-ego in this otherwise factual account, and it is notable that his cowardice is attributed to the fact that, unlike Read, he has a mother and 'never got free of his home thoughts'.

Like most soldiers in all wars, Read was by this stage fighting above all for the men around him. His poem 'My Company' is a eulogy to the intense comradeship and unity forged in the heat of battle and by the shared ordeal of the trenches. He and his men, almost all fellow Yorkshiremen, became 'a body and a soul entire'. 'It is this comradeship alone that makes the army tolerable to me,' he wrote to Evelyn. 'To create a bond between yourself and a body of men, and a bond that will hold at the critical moment, that is work worthy of any man and when done an achievement to be proud of.' Together with his childhood experience of life on a self-sufficient farm, this unanimity had a great influence on his future belief that small units of production could form the basis of a free anarchist society. That this comradeship and unity of purpose did not survive the war was a source of great disillusionment.

If in the raid he had passed one great test, worse was still to come. In September his battalion was moved north from Arras to the Ypres Salient, where the monstrous attritional battle of Passchendaele was still raging. Read was away on leave when his men were thrown into the attack in October and he returned to find them in the thick of the fighting near Polygonveld. Most who were there remembered Passchendaele as their worst experience of the war and Read was no different. In the original version of *Naked Warriors,* later modified by Read, he wrote:

> Arras was a picnic, but Ypres
> That ghastly desolation
> Sank into men's hearts and turned them black
> Cankered them with horror.

Incessant rain and shelling with gas and high explosive had turned the battlefield into a stinking swamp where drowning in shell holes was common. The British generals persisted in their attack despite determined German resistance and escalating carnage. Read's battalion spent weeks cowering in the mud under ceaseless bombardment. By the time they were withdrawn in November, they had lost almost half their strength. 'Life has never seemed so cheap nor nature so mutilated,' he wrote to Evelyn. Morale in the British army was now at its lowest ebb, and Read reported a great growth of pacifist opinion. The promised breakthrough had not been achieved, and tens of thousands had been sacrificed for almost no territorial gain. The rate of attrition was such that Britain was by now running out of men to feed the war machine. In February 1918 Read's battalion was one of many disbanded to reinforce other depleted units. He was assigned to the 2nd Green Howards - a battalion of the regular army. They were deployed in a quiet section of the line in France near St Quentin, close to the old battlefield of the Somme. It was not quiet for long.

    The collapse of Russia's armies after the revolution in 1917 allowed Germany to move huge forces to the western front for what it hoped would be a decisive offensive. The aim was to break the British army and secure victory before America, which had joined the allied side, could bring its might to bear. The attack began on

21st March with the biggest bombardment of the war so far. Under cover of fog, the Germans attacked in massive numbers using new infiltration tactics. Winston Churchill, who was there, called it 'the greatest onslaught in the history of the world'.

Read was caught in the centre of the storm. His account of the desperate defence, 'In Retreat', is one of the finest pieces of writing to come out of the war. It stands comparison with the German classic *Storm of Steel* by Ernst Jünger, who was among the stormtroopers leading the assault. In clear, spare prose it captures without sensationalism the terrible experience of combat against overwhelming odds. Read and his men were repeatedly surrounded and driven out of their defensive positions, 'fighting as I never dreamed we should fight'. Orders from the rear were limited to hysterical appeals to hold on to the last man and they were twice shelled by their own artillery. After the Colonel was wounded, Read took command and led the remnants of the battalion in a desperate fighting retreat, killing hundreds of attackers as they went. At one stage the men had to be held up at revolver point to stop them fleeing in terror. The Germans advanced 40 miles into open country, breaking the deadlock of trench warfare for the first time since 1914 and bringing the allies to the brink of defeat. But thanks to the resistance of men like Read, the line held.

After six days and nights of hell, Read was withdrawn from the fighting. But even then the nightmare was not over. When the Germans attacked again in Flanders in a final doomed attempt to drive the British into the sea, Read's battalion, now a composite of other shattered units, was once more thrown into battle near Ypres. They were 'cruelly smashed' and his best friend, Captain Colin Davidson, was taken prisoner. At least Davidson survived the war. Most of Read's friends did not. He later calculated that, of the hundreds of young soldiers he had known, only a score or so were still alive by the end. No later friendships ever matched the intensity of those forged in battle.

Years afterwards, Read described March 21st as 'a day so vivid and intense that the rest of life has seemed to pivot around it'. Though he had once again proved himself as a soldier – he was awarded the Distinguished Service Order, a medal rarely given to junior officers – the battle was also a moment of political epiphany. If such slaughter could be inflicted by the state, he reasoned, then the state itself was a monster. The book he carried into battle was Henry David Thoreau's *Walden*. For Read in the elation of survival, that transcendental meditation on personal freedom was a perfect antidote to the horrors of war and had a profound impact on his thoughts. 'It all drives me to an individualism, an anarchy which is for each of us to realise,' he told Evelyn. 'A beautiful anarchy, that is my cry'.

By this stage Read was a Captain and had the chance to go for a staff job that would take him out of the front line, if not out of the war. Instead, he applied to be a pilot in the Royal Air Force (RAF), the only place where his chances of being killed were higher, although he would at least escape the squalor of the trenches. But on his return to England the RAF turned him down on health grounds. In September a medical board found that he was suffering from 'debility' and attacks of fainting as a result of the strain of combat. Once again, he had passed the limit of his endurance. Yet for all his disillusion, the contradiction between his political convictions and his commitment as a soldier was still unresolved. He was intent on applying for a permanent commission in the army and went so far as to get a recommendation from his commanding officer. Decades later he described the real horror of war as a 'psychotic state of hallucination' in which you no longer know if you

are sane. It took one final, personal tragedy to wake him from that madness.

By now the war was almost over. Exhausted by the effort of its last failed offensive, the German army was in headlong retreat, reeling under a succession of allied blows. All but forgotten now, this was the greatest victory in the history of the British Army. Read's brother Charlie, recently returned from fighting in Italy, was at the heart of the advance. On 5th October, barely a month before the Armistice, he was killed by machine gun fire while leading his company in the assault on the last defences of the Hindenburg Line at Beaurevoir. Family letters suggest he was keen to be awarded the Military Cross to match his brothers. He was 21 years old. The news of Charlie's death reached Read at an army camp in Middlesbrough and left him distraught. His immediate reaction in poetry, 'Auguries of Life and Death', is full of raw anger, and its attempt to find consolation does not ring true.

The war left Read with 'no visible wounds to lick' and he had gained great self-confidence from his success as a soldier, together with a sense that he had been spared by providence for a reason. His writing had won him an entry into London literary circles, but in the immediate aftermath of the war he found there was little interest in what he had to say about it. After a victory bought at such terrible cost, the idea that it had all been futile was not something Britain wanted to hear. A nation of widows and orphans could not bear the thought that their men had been sacrificed in vain; not until the 1960s did that become the accepted national narrative. Read took a job as a civil servant in the Treasury, but soon switched to the Victoria and Albert Museum, where his career as an art critic began to take off.

Yet he remained haunted by his military experience, and as the shadow of war loomed once again in Europe, he felt compelled to speak out. A key moment was the publication in 1929 of the classic German anti-war novel, *All Quiet on the Western Front* by Erich Maria Remarque. Read was involved in bringing out the translated version and there is a suggestion that he came up with the English title. He felt that the book at last expressed the truth about the war, even though its tone is far removed from that of his own writing at the time. He returned to the subject in poetry in 1933 with 'The End of a War', which provides a mature reflection on his time in the trenches. This was the only First World War poem included in the 1936 *Oxford Book of Modern Verse*. The editor, WB Yeats, rejected the likes of Wilfred Owen on the grounds that 'passive suffering is not a theme for poetry'. In Read's poem, the contrast between the dying German officer who 'fought with gladness' and felt 'the ecstasy of battle' and the disillusion of the surviving Englishman seems a clear expression of his divided self as a pacifist soldier. In a telling review of official war literature in 1935 he strongly defended the reputation of General Hubert Gough, his Army Commander in March 1918. Gough was widely blamed for failing to contain the German push, but Read argued that he should instead be honoured for winning 'the decisive battle of the Great War'.

    It was the outbreak of the Spanish Civil War in 1936 that led Read to express publicly the anarchist convictions that had been born on the blood-soaked battlefields. He was by now one of Britain's foremost public intellectuals, but his advocacy of that most marginal and romantic of political ideologies won little welcome at a time when the only choice seemed to be between parliamentary democracy and the totalitarianism of Hitler or Stalin. For Read though, the lesson of his experience was clear, as he expressed in 1940 in *The Philosophy of Anarchism*:

> There is no problem to which, during the last thirty years, I have given more thought than this problem of war and peace; it has been the obsession of my generation. There is no problem which leads so inevitably to anarchism. Peace is anarchy...War will exist as long as the State exists.

Read saw the Second World War as a grim inevitability, the result of the failure to embrace radical change after 1918. Throughout the conflict, he contributed articles to the anarchist Freedom Press and was outspoken in the defence of anarchists put on trial for inciting soldiers to desert in 1945. But he had no doubt that the Nazis were the far greater evil and he felt great sympathy for the British soldiers facing what he had endured. His eldest son, John, was in the army, though not in a combat unit.

In 1939 he compiled *The Knapsack*, a pocket anthology of prose and verse designed for soldiers to carry into war. In the preface he stresses his conviction that 'the love of glory, even in our materialistic age, is still the main source of virtue. The real good is not done by calculation nor defined by reason, it is an act of courage or of grace.' He also returned to the subject in poetry. 'To a Conscript of 1940' is perhaps his most powerful war poem, capturing perfectly his disillusionment as a soldier:

> We think we gave in vain. The World was not renewed
> There was hope in the homestead and anger in the streets
> But the old world was restored and we returned
> To the dreary field and workshop, and the immemorial
>                                                       feud
>
> Of rich and poor. Our victory was our defeat.

Yet the poem also distils his almost mystical belief that, even though the slaughter had been futile, there was somehow still glory in battle:

> To fight without hope is to fight with grace
> The self reconstructed, the false heart repaired.

This apparent contradiction was the core of Read's war experience and perhaps the hardest for later generations to comprehend. He regarded war as the ultimate evil, yet the values he saw demonstrated – comradeship, self-sacrifice, unity of purpose – filled him with immense hope for the future of humankind. This 'paradox of hope in the midst of despair' convinced him that, if they could escape the tyranny of the state, men could build a free and equal society. Somehow the romanticism rooted in his idyllic rural childhood had survived the horror of the trenches.

The terrible climax of the Second World War reinforced his pacifist and anarchist convictions. The poem '1945' surely addresses the nuclear destruction of Hiroshima and Nagasaki. His children run towards him on a beach:

> But I saw only the waves behind them
> Cold, salt and disastrous
> Lift their black banners and break
> Endlessly, without resurrection.

In 1960 Read was a founding member of the Committee of 100, the militant wing of the nuclear disarmament movement. But he resigned a year later over a protest at an airbase that he thought came too close to violence. Unlike most revolutionaries, he was adamant in his rejection of the use of force, advocating instead a Gandhian approach. And unlike most pacifists, his conviction was based on experience of war at its worst.

A century after it began, the First World War is almost universally remembered in Britain as a disastrous and futile conflict, particularly in contrast to the Second World War. The image of pointless slaughter in the mud is deeply engrained in the national mythology. But that view only became generally accepted in the 1960s. Read knew it right from the start. That he fought anyway, and fought so well, was a contradiction he fully recognised, but never entirely resolved. Defenders of Britain's participation today justify it in terms of the defence of democracy, despite the fact that few of the men who fought, and no women, had the vote in 1914. In any case that argument would cut no ice with Read. For him, true democracy meant workers' control, mutual aid and the disappearance of the state. His hope at the time that the war would be ended by a workers' revolution may appear naïve – but that is exactly what happened in Russia, albeit with eventually disastrous results. Germany almost went the same way, and the Ottoman and Austro-Hungarian empires collapsed.

Read's greatest disillusion was that all that blood and sacrifice had been in vain. If only the cause and outcome had lived up to the values shown by the men who fought. But that disillusion never gave way to despair, and he kept his promise to fight for peace when peace came. In some ways his entire career as a writer and critic can be seen as part of that struggle – a quest to redeem mankind and transform society with education and art, rather than bullets and bombs.

*Further Reading*

- David Goodway (ed.), *Herbert Read Reassessed* (Liverpool: Liverpool University Press, 1998)
- James King, *The Last Modern: A Life of Herbert Read* (London: Weidenfeld and Nicolson, 1990)
- Michael Paraskos, *Herbert Read: Art and Idealism* (Mitcham: Orage Press, 2014)
- Michael Paraskos (ed.), *Re-Reading Read: New Views on Herbert Read* (London: Freedom Press, 2007)

# FIRST WORLD WAR POEMS AND ILLUSTRATIONS

**AEROPLANES**

A dragonfly
in the flecked grey sky.

Its silvered planes
break the wide and still
harmony of space.

Around it shells
flash
their fumes
burgeoning to blooms
smoke-lilies that float
along the sky.

Among them darts
a dragonfly.

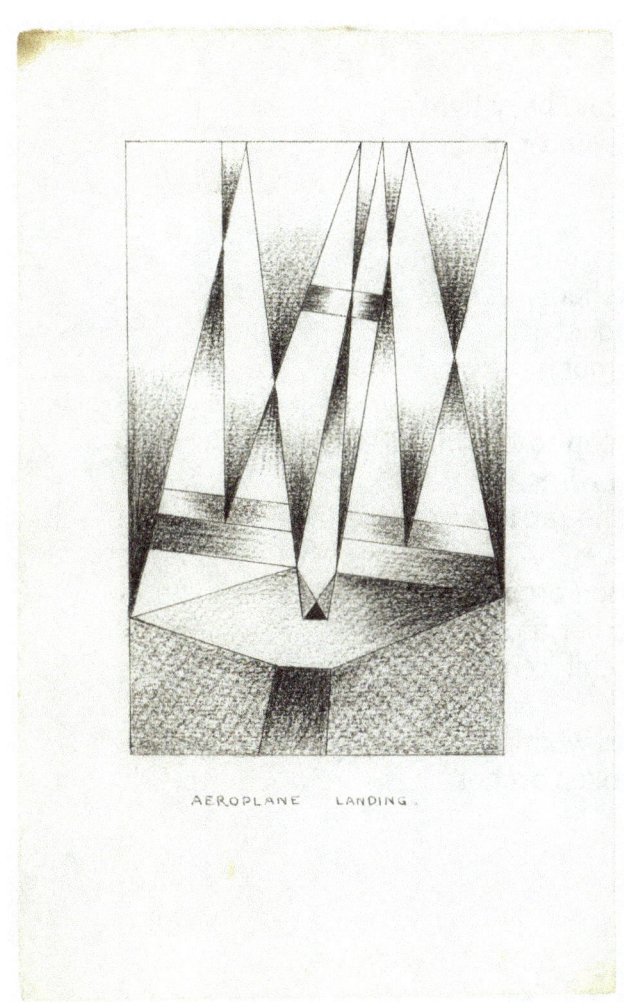
AEROPLANE LANDING.

**YPRES**

1

With a chill and hazy light
the sun of a winter noon
swills
thy ruins.

Thy ruins etched
in silver silhouettes
against a turquoise sky.

Lank poles leap to the infinite
their broken wires
tossed like the rat-locks of Maenades.

And Desolation broods over all
gathering to her lap
her leprous children.

The sparrows whimper
amid the broken arches.

2

Sunset
licks the ruins
with vermeil flames.
the flames rise and fall

against the dusking sky –
against the dusking sky
flames fall and die.

Heaped in the black night
are the grey ashes
of desolation.

But even now the moon
blooms
like a cankered rose
and with a soft passionate light
kisses
the wan harmonies of ruin.

## THE AUTUMN OF THE WORLD

As a host of blood-flecked clouds
skim the golden sky
and melt into the vermilioned vastness
there comes borne on a wind
from the infinite womb of chaos
the dank wafture of decay.

Over the eternal waters of the sea
that weep and find no solace for their cares
lethargic vultures flock and swirl
and fill the echoes with their gloomy songs.

Hot winds from tropic zones
betray
the transient things of Earth.
The last yellow leaves fall
on the iridescent sward.
The wind dies
and the Summer voices are forever still.

## CHAMP DE MANOEUVRES

This hill indents my soul
so that I sag
like a silver mist about its flanks.

I dwell
in the golden setting of the sun
while on the plain
the illumin'd mists invade
leaf-burden'd trees.

And then
the silent tides of melting light
assail the hill, imbue
my errant soul.

The empty body broods
one with the inanimate rocks.

The last rays are fierce and irritant.
Then on the lonely hill my body wakes
and gathers to its shell my startled soul.

JACKSON'S 3/9.

[It's not so comfortable as it looks.]

## MOVEMENT OF TROOPS

We entrain in open trucks
and soon glide away
from the plains of Artois.

With a wake of white smoke
we plunge
down dark avenues of silent trees.

A watcher sees
our red light gleam
occasionally.

## NAKED WARRIORS (1919)

*Preface:*

I would like to speak for a new generation to the following effect:

We, who in manhood's dawn have been compelled to care not a damn for life or death, now care less still for the convention of glory and the intellectual apologies for what can never be to us other than a riot of ghastliness and horror, of inhumanity and negation. May we, therefore, for the sake of life itself, be resolved to live with a cleaner and more direct realisation of natural values. May we be unafraid of our frank emotions, and may we maintain a callous indifference to the falsely-artistic prettifying of life. Then, as the reflex of such stern activity, may we strive to create a beauty where hitherto it has had no absolute existence. From the sickness of life revealed let us turn with glad hearts to the serenity of some disinterested beauty. In that way we may so progress that our ethical rage gives us duly an aesthetic sanction.

## PARODY OF A FORGOTTEN BEAUTY

War through my soul has driven
Its jagged blades :
The riven
Dream fades –
So you'd better grieve, heart, in the gathering night,
Grieve, heart, in the loud twilight.

## KNEESHAW GOES TO WAR

*Reule thyself, that other folk may rede
And trouthe shall delivere, it is no drede.*

- Geoffrey Chaucer

1

Ernest Kneeshaw grew
In the forest of his dreams
Like a woodland flower whose anaemic petals
Need the sun.

Life was a far perspective
Of high black columns
Flanking, arching and encircling him.
He never, even vaguely, tried to pierce
The gloom about him,
But was content to contemplate
His finger-nails and wrinkled boots.

He might at least have perceived
A sexual atmosphere;
But even when his body burned and urged
Like the buds and roots around him,
Abashed by the will-less promptings of his flesh,
He continued to contemplate his feet.

## 2

Kneeshaw went to war.
On bleak moors among harsh fellows
They set about with much painstaking
To straighten his drooping back:

But still his mind reflected things
Like a cold steel mirror – emotionless;
Yet in reflecting he became accoplished
And, to some extent,
Divested of ancestral gloom.
Then Kneeshaw crossed the sea.

At Boulougne
He cast a backward glance across the harbours
And saw there a forest of assembled masts and rigging.
Like the sweep from a releas'd dam,
His thoughts flooded unfamiliar paths:

*This forest was congregated*
*From various climates and strange seas :*
*Hadn't each ship some separate memory*
*Of sunlit scenes or arduous waters?*
*Didn't each bring in the high glamour*
*Of conquering force?*
*Wasn't the forest-gloom of their assembly*
*A body built of living cells,*
*Of personalities and experiences*
    *-   A witness of heroism*
*Co-existent with man?*

*And that dark forest of his youth –
Couldn't he liberate the black columns
Flanking, arching, encircling him with dread?
Couldn't he let them spread from his vision like a fleet
Taking the open sea,
Disintegrating into light and colour and the fragrance of
    winds?
And perhaps to some thought they would return
Laden with strange merchandise –
And with the passing thought
Pass unregretted into far horizons.*

*These were Kneeshaw's musings
Whilst he yet dwelt in the romantic fringes.*

3

Then, with many other men,
He was transported in a cattle-truck
To the scene of war.

For a while chance was kind
Save for an inevitable
Searing of the mind
But later Kneeshaw's war
Became intense.
The ghastly desolation
Sank into men's hearts and turned them black –
Cankered them with horror.
Kneeshaw felt himself

A cog in some great evil engine,
Unwilling, but revolv'd tempestuously
By unseen springs.
He plunged with listless mind
Into the black horror.

4

There are a few left who will find it hard to forget
Polygonveld.
The earth was scarr'd and broken
By torrents of plunging shells;
Then was'd and sodden with autumnal rains.
And Polygonbeke
(Perhaps a rippling stream
In the days of Kneeshaw's gloom)
Spread itself like a fatal quicksand, -
A sucking, clutching death.
They had to be across the beke
And in their line before dawn.
A man who was marching by Kneeshaw's side
Hesitated in the middle of the mud,
And slowly sank, weighted down by equipment and arms.
He cried for help;
Rifles were stretched to him;
He clutched and they tugged,
But slowly he sank.
His terror grew –
Grew visibly when the viscous ooze
Reached his neck.

And there he seemed to stick,
Sinking no more.
They could not dig him out –
The oozing mud would flow back again.

The dawn was very near.

An officer shot him through the head:
Not a neat job – the revolver
Was too close.

5

Then the dawn came, silver on the wet brown earth.

Kneeshaw found himself in the second wave:
The unseen springs revolved the cog
Through all the mutations of that storm of death.
He started when he heard them cry 'Dig in!'
He had to think and couldn't for a while.
Then he seized a pick from the nearest man
And clawed passionately upon the churned earth.
With satisfaction his pick
Cleft the skull of a buried man.
Kneeshaw tugged the clinging pick,
Saw its burden and shrieked.

For a second or two he was impotent
Vainly trying to recover his will, but his senses prevailing.

Then mercifully

A hot blast and riotous detonation
Hurled his mangled body
Into the beautiful peace of coma.

6

There came a day when Kneeshaw,
Minus a leg, on crutches,
Stalked the woods and hills of his native land.
And on the hills he would sing this war-song:

*The forest gloom breaks:*
*The wild black masts*
*Seaward sweep on adventurous ways:*
*I grip my crutches and keep*
*A lonely view.*

*I stand on this hill and accept*
*The pleasure my flesh dictates*
*I count not kisses nor take*
*Too serious a view of tobacco.*

*Judas no doubt was right*
*In a mental sort of way:*
*For he betrayed another and so*
*With purpose was self-justified.*
*But I delivered my body to fear –*
*I was a bloodier fool than he.*

*I stand on this hill and accept*
*The flowers at my feet and the deep*

*Beauty of the still tarn;*
*Chance that gave me a crutch and a view*
*Gave me these.*

*The soul is not a dogmatic affair*
*Like manliness, colour, and light;*
*But these essentials there be:*
*To speak truth and so rule oneself*
*That other folk may rede.*

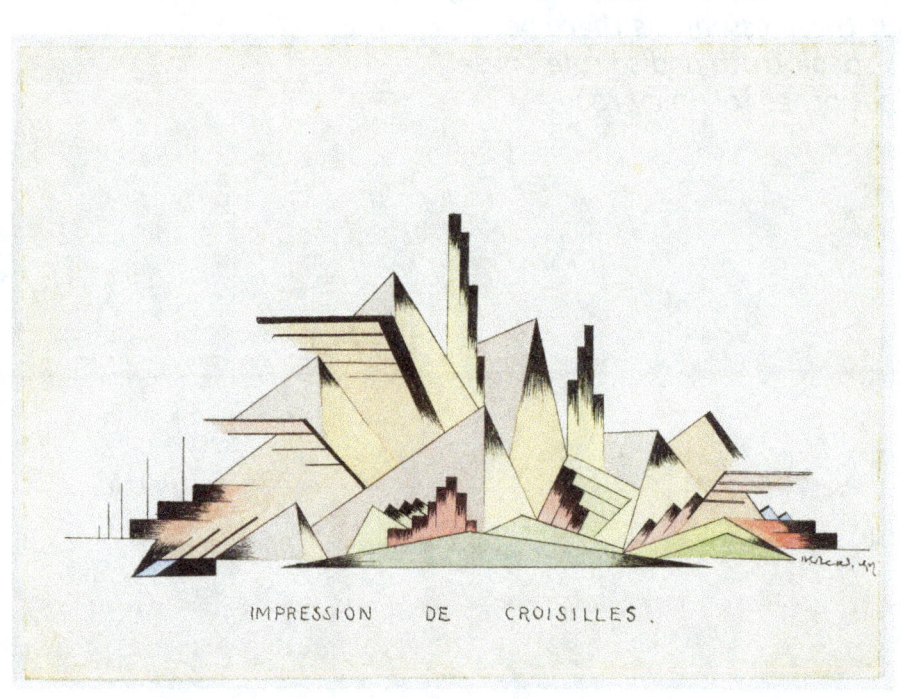

# THE SCENE OF WAR

*And perhaps some outer horror,*
*some hideousness to stamp beauty*
*a mark*
*on our hearts.*
                              *- H.D.*

I.   VILLAGES DÉMOLIS

The villages are strewn
in red and yellow heaps of rubble:

Here and there
interior walls
lie upturned and interrogate the skies amazedly.

Walls that once held
within their cubic confines
a soul that now lies strewn
in red and yellow
heaps of rubble.

## II.    THE CRUCIFIX

His body is smashed
through the belly and chest
the head hangs lopsided
from one nail'd hand.

Emblem of agony
we have smashed you!

## III.  FEAR

Fear is a wave
beating through the air
and on taut nerves impinging
till there it wins
vibrating chords.

All goes well
so long as you tune the instrument
to stimulate composure.

(So you will become
a gallant gentleman.)

But when the strings are broken
then you will grovel on the earth
and your rabbit eyes
will fill with the fragments of your shatter'd soul.

IV.   THE HAPPY WARRIOR

His wild heart beats with painful sobs
his strain'd hands clench an ice-cold rifle
his aching jaws grip a hot parch'd tongue
his wide eyes search unconsciously.

He cannot shriek.

Bloody saliva
dribbles down his shapeless jacket.

I saw him stab
and stab again
a well-killed Boche.

this is the happy warrior,
this is he....

## V.   LIEDHOLZ

When I captured Liedholz
I had a blacken'd face
like a nigger's
and my teeth like white mosaics shone.

We met in the night at half-past one
between the lines
Liedholz shot at me
and I at him;
in the ensuing tumult he surrendered to me.

Before we reached our wire
he told me he had a wife and three children.
In the dug-out we gave him a whiskey.
Going to the Brigade with my prisoner at dawn
the early sun made the land delightful
and larks rose singing from the plain.

In broken French we discussed
Beethoven, Nietzsche and the International.

He was a professor
Living at Spandau
and not too intelligible.

But my black face and nigger's teeth
amused him.

## VI.  THE REFUGEES

Mute figures with bowed heads
They travel along the road:
Old women, incredibly old
and a hand-cart of chattels.

They do not weep:
their eyes are too raw for tears.

Past them have hastened
processions of retreating gunteams
baggage-wagons and swift horsemen.
Now they struggle along
with the rearguard of a broken army.

We shall hold the enemy towards nightfall
and they will move
mutely into the dark behind us,
only the creaking cart
disturbing their sorrowful serenity.

## VII.  MY COMPANY

*Foule! Ton âme entière est debout dans mon corps.*

- Jules Romains

I

You became
in many acts and quiet observances
A body and a soul, entire.

I cannot tell
what time your life became mine:
perhaps when one summer night
we halted on the roadside
in the starlight only
and you sang your sad home-songs
dirges which I standing outside you
coldly condemned.

Perhaps, one night, descending cold
when rum was mighty acceptable
and my doling gave birth to sensual gratitude.

And then our fights: we've fought together
compact, unanimous
and I have felt the pride of leadership.

In many acts and quiet observances

you absorbed me:
Until one day I stood eminent
and I saw you gather'd round me
uplooking
and about you a radiance that seemed to beat
with variant glow and to give
grace to our unity.

But, God! I know that I'll stand
someday in the loneliest wilderness
someday my heart will cry
for the soul that has been, but that now
is scatter'd with the winds,
deceased and devoid.

I know that I'll wander with a cry:
'O beautiful men, O men I loved
O whither are you gone, my company?'

## 2

My men go wearily
with their monstrous burdens.
They bear wooden planks
and iron sheeting
through the area of death.

When a flare curves through the sky
they rest immobile.

Then on again
Sweating and blaspheming –
'Oh, bloody Christ!'

My men, my modern Christs
your bloody agony confronts the world.

3

A man of mine
      lies on the wire.
It is death to fetch his soulless corpse.


A man of mine
      lies on the wire;
And he will rot
and first his lips
the worms will eat.
It is not thus I would have him kiss'd
but with the warm passionate lips
of his comrade here.

4

I can assume
a giant attitude and godlike mood
and then detachedly regard
all riots, conflicts and collisions.
The men I've lived with
lurch suddenly into a far perspective:
They distantly gather like a dark cloud of birds
in the autumn sky.

Urged by some unanimous
volition or fate
Clouds clash in opposition:
The sky quivers, the dead descend;
earth yawns.

They are all of one species.

From my giant attitude
in godlike mood
I laugh till space is filled
with hellish merriment.

Then again I assume
my human docility
bow my head
and share their doom.

## VIII.  THE EXECUTION OF CORNELIUS VANE

*Le combat spirituel est aussi brutal que la
bataille d'hommes; mais la vision de la
justice est le plaisir de Dieu seul.*

- Arthur Rimbaud

Arraign'd before his worldly gods
He would have said:
'I, Cornelius Vane,
A fly in the sticky web of life,
Shot away my right index finger.

I was alone, on sentry, in the chill twilight after dawn,
And the act cost me a bloody sweat.
Otherwise the cost was trivial – they had no evidence.
And I lied to the wooden fools who tried me.
When I returned from hospital
They made me a company cook:
I peel potatoes and other men fight.'

For nearly a year Cornelius peeled potatoes
And his life was full of serenity.
Then the enemy broke our line
And their hosts spread over the plains
Like unleash'd beads.
Every man was taken –
Shoemakers, storemen, grooms –

And arms were given them
That they might stem the oncoming host.

Cornelius held out his fingerless hand
And remarked that he couldn't shoot.
'But you can stab,' the sergeant said,
So he fell in with the rest, and, a little group,
They marked away towards the enemy.

After an hour they halted for a rest.
They were already in the fringe of the fight:
Desultory shells fell about them,
And past them retreating gunteams
Galloped in haste.
But they must go on.

Wounded stragglers came down the road,
Haggard and limping
Their arms and equipment tossed away.
Cornelius Vane saw them, and his heart was beating wildly,
For he must go on.

At the next halt
He went aside to piss,
And whilst away a black shell
Burst near him:
Hot metal shrieked past his face;
Bricks and earth descended like hail,
And the acrid stench of explosive filled his nostrils.

Cornelius pitched his body to the ground

And crouched in trembling fear.
Another shell came singing overhead,
Nowhere near.

But Cornelius sprang to his feet, his pale face set.
He willed nothing, saw nothing, only before him
Were the free open fields:
To the fields he ran.

He was still running when he began to perceive
The tranquillity of the fields
And the battle distant.
Away in the north-east were men marching on a road;
Behind were the smoke-puffs of shrapnel,
And in the west the sun declining
In a sky of limpid gold.

When night came finally
He had reached a wood.
In the thickness of the trees
The cold wind was excluded,
And here he slept a few hours.

In the early dawn
The chill mist and heavy dew
Pierced his bones and awakened him.
There was no sound of battle to be heard.

In the open fields again
The sun shone sickly through the mist
And the dew was icy to the feet.

So Cornelius ran about in that white night,
The sun's wan glare his only guide.

Coming to a canal
He ran up and down like a dog
Deliberating where to cross.
One way he saw a bridge
Loom vaguely, but approaching
He heard voices and turned about.
He went far the other way,
But growing tired before he found a crossing,
Plunged into the icy water and swam.
The water gripped with agony;
His clothes sucked the heavy water,
And as he ran again
Water oozed and squelched from his boots
His coat dripped and his teeth chattered.

He came to a farm.
Approaching cautiously, he found it deserted.
Within he discarded his sopping uniform, dried himself and
    donned
Mufti he found in a cupboard.
Dark mouldy bread and bottled cider he also found
And was refreshed.
Whilst he was eating,
Suddenly,
Machine-guns opened fire not far away,
And their harsh throbbing
Darkened his soul with fear.

The sun was more golden now,
And as he went –
Always going west –
The mist grew thin.

About noon,
As he skirted the length of the wood
The warmth had triumphed and the spring day was beautiful.
Cornelius perceived with a new joy
Pale anemones and violets of the wood,
And wished that he might ever
Exist in the perception of these woodland flowers
And the shafts of yellow light that pierced
The green dusk.

Two days later
He entered a village and was arrested.
He was hungry, and the peace of the fields
Dissipated the terror that had been the strength of his will.

He was charged with desertion
And eventually tried by court-martial.

The evidence was heavy against him,
And he was mute in his own defence.
A dumb anger and a despair
Filled his soul.

He was found guilty.
Sentence: to suffer death by being shot.

The sentence duly confirmed,
One morning at dawn they led him forth.
He saw a party of his own regiment,
With rifles looking very sad.
The morning was bright, and as they tied
The cloth over his eyes, he said to the assembly:
'What wrong have I done that I should leave these:
The bright sun rising
And the birds that sing?'

## AUGURIES OF LIFE AND DEATH

*Written in memory of Charles Read, Lieutenant of the Yorkshire Regiment, born 29 April 1897. Killed in action at Beaurevoir in France, 5 October 1918*

1

The autumn leaves were an augury
And seemed to intend
As they yellowly drooped in the languid air
That life was a fragile mood and death
A tremendous despair.

The yellow leaves fell
Like slow tears of gold on the face of the day:
They fell to the earth with a faint sad sigh.

They sighed
As the feet of the passers-by
Crushed them into the moist black soil:
They sighed when the gentle wind
Lifted them along the way.

In the park
Old men swept the dead things in a heap to burn:
Their last fragrance
Floated about the naked trees.

I thought as the women walked in the moist still day

Wearing yellow chrysanthemums in their coats
A chrysanthemum was
A pale dishevelled emblem of death.

The sun
Was a silver pervasion across the sky:
From the sky
The dead leaves fell.

2

Some well-meaning fool
called him an unconscious Sidney
proudly dying in the surge of battle.
Many said
he paid the supreme sacrifice...

Let us be frank for once:
Such foisted platitudes
cannot console sick hearts.
Rather this alone is clear:
He was a delightful youth
irradiating joy, peculiarly loved
by hundreds of his fellows.
The impulse of his living
left a wake of laughter
and happiness in the hearts of sad men.

Then this glad progression
is suddenly cut short
annihilated.

We hear
he was killed in action, leading his men ...
In a moment that life and its radiance
went out like a blown flame.

No natural logic can explain
that harsh departure and our dark void.
The knotted bitterness grips tight
I curse the fate that sent us
a tortured species down the torrent of life
soul-exposed to insensate shores
and the dark fall of death.

Yet in the scene of life
a consolation I can find.
All things do cry
vain is rebellion.
Is not the gargoyle leer of fate
in all its impassive cruelty
known too well
for any man to rebel?
The tendrils of our intensest emotions
are torn by its inane force
and strewn in bleeding death.
But no devastation can
utterly kill:
in the burnt blackness of earth
built from invisible beginnings
womb-warmth will engender
an animate thing.

So we might make his short delightful life
an instance of those beauties that adorn
tragically the earth with flowers
heroes and valiant hearts.

This flower hold dear
till the years evolve in their callous recession
a memorized beauty.

3

All the world is wet with tears
and droops its languid life
in sympathy.
But death is beautiful with pride: the trees
are golden lances whose brave array
assails the sadness of the day.
They do not meet
fate with an angry tumult:
Serene they stay
austerely dying day by day:
Their golden lances imperceptibly fade
into the sleep of winter, their victory made
in the hearts of men.

# FROM THE CONTRARY EXPERIENCE: AUTOBIOGRAPHIES
(published 1963)

# THE IMPACT OF WAR

At the outbreak of war in 1914 I was already in a military camp. This was not the outcome of any immediate patriotic zeal on my part, but was to some extent a consequence of my patriotic past. A year or two before I became an undergraduate, and while still contemplating the possibility of a medical career, I had joined the local territorial unit of the Royal Army Medical Corps in the vain hope that I should acquire some practical experience. By the time I reached the University, this had become a meaningless and arduous engagement, to which I was nevertheless bound for a period of years. But at the University there was an Officers' Training Corps, and I eagerly seized the opportunity to transfer my military bond to this more agreeable branch of the service. It is true that as time went on and my political ideas developed, I had certain qualms of conscience. But very few of those who joined the OTC in those days had any serious motive. War was considered as a very remote contingency, and meanwhile here was an open-air club, with possibilities of friendship and youthful enterprise, and an annual camp which was in effect a free holiday for many who could not otherwise afford one. I was not interested in sport of any kind, and the OTC provided me with my one physical diversion. I enjoyed the game very much.

    There, happily at play, I was caught by the war. In the years that followed I was often to ask myself what I would have done if I had been a free agent. Politically I was a pacifist, and regarded the war as a conflict between rival imperial powers which would bring destruction to the peoples engaged. I hoped that the war would be stopped by international working-class action, and the failure of the responsible leaders to bring about a stoppage was my first lesson in political disillusionment. But fundamentally - that is to say, ethically - I could not claim to be a pacifist. It must be remembered that in 1914 our conception of war was completely unreal. We had vague childish memories of the Boer War, and from these and from a general diffusion of Kiplingesque sentiments, we managed to infuse into war a decided element of adventurous romance. War still appealed to the imagination. To this romantic illusion must be added, in my own case, a state of uncertainty about my future. Though I was ambitious and full of determination, I had no precise career marked out: I was to be a free-lance of some sort, and a free-lance finds a very appropriate place in an army. The war meant a decision: a crystallization of vague projects: an immediate acceptance of the challenge of life. I did not hesitate.

    I received a commission within six months and was posted to a battalion of the Green Howards, my local North Riding regiment, then training in Dorset. This battalion had, like most of the newly-formed units, a nucleus of regular officers drawn from one of the first-line battalions, together with a few reservists, but the bulk of the officers were recruits from the OTC. It happened that a considerable group in my particular battalion came from Eton (including two masters, Young and Slater); and practically all the others were from public schools. I had, therefore, stumbled into a very select and at first very uncongenial coterie. It must be remembered that I had not hitherto been outside my provincial fastness: but it was not so much my rawness (concealed as it was by my natural diffidence) as my incredible naïveté which was at fault. I will give two examples. I had become a regular reader of *The New Age*, at that time the most independent and lively periodical being published. The officers' mess occupied a building ordinarily used by the local masonic lodge, and there we had an anteroom where all the usual magazines and newspapers were available. They were displayed on a green-baize table, and there, when I had read it, I left my copy of *The New Age*. I was seated deep in an armchair one afternoon when the senior subaltern, traditionally responsible for the social conduct of the junior subalterns, came up to the table and casually picked up *The New Age*. He looked at it for a minute or two and slowly the colour deepened in his rather florid face. He turned suddenly to address the room, and holding the paper up between his finger and thumb as though it was unclean, he shouted in a loud voice: 'Who brought this bloody rag into the mess?' I wish I could say that I sprang to my feet to defend my intellectual interests; but alas, I was not so naïve as that. I shrank still deeper into my chair and watched the angry senior subaltern stalk out in disgust, throwing the offensive periodical into the waste-paper basket as he passed. I had learned my lesson, and in the future read *The New Age* in the privacy of my tent or cubicle.

    The other incident was similar and occurred shortly afterwards. The mess was actually the only place where, that bitter winter, one could read in comfort - I was still under canvas. One Sunday afternoon I took down with me a book I had just bought - Butler's *Erewhon Revisited* - and was soon absorbed in it. The mess was, as I had anticipated, nearly empty, but presently Captain Slater, the Eton master already mentioned, came in and, passing behind my chair, observed the title of my book. 'O God! O Montreal!' he cried, 'that I should find someone reading Sam Butler in the British Army.' He was genuinely amused and interested, and though we were too disparate in age and temperament ever to become close friends, a sympathetic bond did henceforth exist between us.

But that, too, was a lesson. So long as we remained in England I confined my mess reading to the *Tatler* and the *Bystander* and other periodicals of the kind which were the only literary recreations of the majority of His Majesty's officers. When we reached the Front the situation changed, in this as in many other respects.

Meanwhile I was reacting to a new and unexpected mode of life. For the first time I was compelled to be continuously active in the open air, and though the strain was great, there was exhilaration in meeting it. For the first time, again, I was thrown against all sorts and conditions of men: on the one side I had to adapt myself to the manner and habits of my fellow-officers, most of whom came from an entirely different and wealthier social world; and on the other side I became personally responsible for a platoon of soldiers, the majority of them toughened in the mines and factories of Durham and North Yorkshire. I found the officers more difficult than the men. The colonel was comprehensible: he was an English gentleman of a type I had been familiar with in my childhood, a good solider in wartime and a good squire in peacetime; and there were two or three other regulars who were at any rate efficient and experienced. But the majority - young subalterns fresh from Sandhurst and the public-school boys already mentioned, struck me as snobbish and intolerant, as trying to import into the Army the prefectorial spirit which they had acquired at school. Luckily I was not alone outside this predominant group, and some half a dozen of us managed to make our own society.

This sense of disunity lasted during the training period in England. In France the pressure of events, particularly the test of danger, quickly changed the atmosphere. Social values yielded to realistic values. In England we had unconsciously accepted the habit of command and the air of superiority which environment and education had conferred on the sons of the élite. Now we discovered that something else mattered more: that irreducible element of personality which is the raw material of education and the principle of growth persisting through every environment. It is my conviction that education and environment cannot change this innate spirit of an individual. Education can adapt the individual to his environment: it can explain life and reality to him and thus enable him to face them more skilfully with the gifts with which he is naturally endowed. It can also make him more conscious of the scope or limitation of these gifts. In the same way war, which is so often made the melodramatic agent of changes in character, does not affect the inherent quality of the person. As the months went by, I was to see all the proud pretensions which men had acquired from a conventional environment sink into insignificance before the basic facts of body and spirit. In my own case I was to discover, with a sense of self-confidence wholly new to me, that I could endure the experience of war, even at its worst. This is far from claiming that I was fearless: the first days in the trenches, the first bombardment or attack, was a draining sickness of the spirit. But I presently recovered, as from a plunge into a cold sea. What I found most difficult to accustom myself to, even after months at the Front, was the sight of human blood, and the stiff horror of a human corpse. That one does eventually get used to such things does not necessarily mean a deadening of the sensibility; but when an experience is repeated often enough, one has to rationalize it - in other words, make one's philosophy fit the facts.

 I do not intend to give a detailed account of the four and a half years I spent in the Army: it is the totality of the experience which has significance for my present purpose. But there are two incidents which I have related with some attempt at an analysis of my accompanying feelings while they are still fresh in my mind - a raid which took place in the early summer of 1917 and the retreat of the Fifth Army from St Quentin in March, 1918. The first of these narratives was published in 1930 in a small collection of prose pieces which I called *Ambush*; the second was written in 1919, but first published by Leonard and Virginia Woolf at the Hogarth Press six years later.

 These short narratives are reproduced as separate chapters in the following pages. To the best of my ability 'The Raid', which will not be found to deviate in any essential point from the briefer account given in the War Diary, adequately represents for me the subjective experience of war. The raid itself was, of course, a comparatively intense moment in the general course of that experience, and there were long stretches of boredom and inaction which should no doubt be reckoned as part of the total impact. But in so far as fear is the core of that experience, and the phenomenon about which those who have not experienced war betray the most curiosity, the analysis given in this narrative is the only evidence I have to offer. Whether we reach the reality by analysis, which is a subjective instrument, is another question; but in so far as the events can speak for themselves, they do so in 'The Retreat', which I have tried to make an objective record.

If I had entered the war in a certain spirit of adventurous acceptance, as it was prolonged year after year it began to conflict with the impatient spirit of youth. One week in the trenches was sufficient to strip war of its lingering traces of romance: there was nothing, in the Ypres Salient where I first went into the line, but primitive filth, lice, boredom and death. Even the novelty of the experience, in such circumstances, is no palliative. But after weeks, and then months, and finally years of such a life, with no moral sanction to support the spirit, no fervour or enthusiasm, no hatred of the enemy, the whole business became fantastically unreal, a monstrous nightmare from which one could not awake. It should be remembered that a modern army is largely made up of young civilians without political experience, and the propaganda which is designed to inspire them (and perhaps does inspire them for a time) soon wears thin against the crude realities of war. If only, I used to think, we poor bloody soldiers could walk out, walk home, and leave the politicians to make the best of a quarrel which we did not understand and which had no interest for us! But though these were the sentiments of nine men out of ten, there was no possibility of proceeding to action. A soldier is part of a machine: once the machine is in movement, he functions as part of that machine, or simply gets killed. There is very little scope for individual initiative, for non-co-operation. It is true that one need not - and I did not - industriously strive to kill. During the whole war I never deliberately or consciously killed an individual man, with the possible exception of the one who was accompanying the German officer in the raid I am going to describe. I fired in self-defence, at advancing masses of men; but I never in cold blood selected my mark, with the intention of bringing to an end a human life. In April, 1918, when on a daylight 'contact' patrol with two of my men, we suddenly confronted, round some mound or excavation, a German patrol of the same strength. We were perhaps twenty yards from each other, fully visible. I waved a weary hand, as if to say: 'What is the use of killing each other?' The German officer seemed to understand, and both parties turned and made their way back to their own trenches. Reprehensible conduct, no doubt, but in April, 1918, the war-weariness of the infantry was stronger than its pugnacity, on both sides of the line.

  The impact of war on my sensibility is best revealed in the change which came to my writing during the period. As I have already said, it was a change of content rather than of technique. In 1915 I was already writing in the imagist manner, and from the Front I sent to *The Gryphon*, the student's magazine at Leeds, various contributions of which the earliest must have been written within a few weeks of my war experience. They are, as imagist poems should be, coldly objective. The following is an impression of Ypres:

> *With a chill and hazy light*
> *the sun of a winter noon*
> *swills*
> *thy ruins.*
>
> *Thy ruins etched*
> *in silver silhouettes*

*against a turquoise sky.*

*Lank poles leap to the infinite,
their broken wires
tossed like the rat-locks of Maenades.*

*And Desolation broods over all,
gathering to her lap
her leprous children.*

*The sparrows whimper
amid the broken arches.*

Besides these poems, some short prose sketches in a 'Zarathustran' style called 'Fables from Flanders', were published during 1916. They are still very idealistic, but a realistic note is creeping in, and towards the end of 1916 I find two poems which I called 'Truth for a Change - an Epilogue to the Fables'. In 1919 I apparently thought they were too sentimental to be included in *Naked Warriors,* but I reproduce one of them now as a contrast to the poem already quoted:

*Such a lad as Harry was
Isn't met with every day.
He walked the land like a god,
Exulting in energy,
Care-free,
His eyes a blue smile
Beneath his yellow curling locks;
And you'd wonder where a common labourer got*

*Those deep Rossetti lips
And finely carven nose ...
I saw him stretch his arms
Languid as a dozing panther,
His face full to the clean sky -
When a blasted sniper laid him low:
He fell limp on the muddy boards
And left us all blaspheming.*

I do not suggest that from a literary point of view such relatively crude and sentimental realism is an improvement on the earlier idealism: indeed, if there is any difference of merit, I am inclined to think that the Ypres poem is better than 'Truth for a Change'. But I should not have thought so in 1916 - much less so in 1917 or 1918. My experience, that is to say, was modifying my literary values, and not altogether for the good. It is still a common assumption - Mr Desmond MacCarthy makes it as I write this chapter - that generous feelings and humane sentiments are more important in poetry than what he calls 'tessellating together unexpected words'. It depends on what Mr MacCarthy means by his derogatory phrase; but in fact poetry is made with words and cannot be made without a fine sense of the right words. Can Mr MacCarthy discover much 'thought and feeling' in 'Kubla Khan'? Poetry, it would seem from this supreme example, can get along with a minimum of sentiment, provided it has a sufficiency of sensibility. But this is not to deny that good poetry can be made out of emotional situations, and in so far as the war induced me to write about emotional situations, it meant an enlargement of my literary experience. But it does not need a war to effect that change in a poet: I should have been brought to it by the impact of life itself.

The war did, of course, broaden in an altogether unexpected fashion my human contacts - far more than any school or university could have done. As the war developed, I found in my fellow-officers a rough equivalent of the society of a university, but more diverse, and deepened and concentrated by the common sharing of dangerous purposes. I had such friends then as I had never had before and have never had since - friends with whom one lived in a complete communal bond of thoughts as well as goods. When peace came, and the bond was destroyed, we drifted apart, back to the alien ways of our different social levels, our different environments and careers. Perhaps most significantly, we lost our masculine exclusiveness.

The most broadening of contacts was, however, that with the rank and file. I can only speak for the infantry, and I only speak of the infantry at war, away from the barracks and parade ground. Then between the company officer and his men there is every opportunity for the development of a relationship that abolishes all class distinctions and that can have a depth of understanding and sympathy for which I know no parallel in civilian life. Unfortunately the word 'leader' now belongs to the ideology of fascism, and in its blustering, commanding sense it was never applicable to a boyish officer in his early twenties, in charge of sixty or more men, many of whom would be much older and more experienced (now it may be different for there is more uniformity of age in a conscript army). The relationship was much more like that of a priest to his parish: for the company officer was the medium of communication with higher authority, one who interpreted the orders and strategy laid down by that authority, one who was therefore the ear and the voice of his group. Within the group he was responsible for the material welfare and comfort of his men - their food and billets, their health, their correspondence, and he it was who communicated with their relatives in case of death. In the trenches a platoon officer would often be isolated for many days with his men, and away from the rest of the officers; his closest companions were at all times his sergeant, his batman and his runner. It was only the social misfit, the public-school snob or worse the snob who came from the fringes of the working-classes, who could not develop a relationship of trust and even of intimacy with his men.

During the war I used to feel that this comradeship which had developed among us would lead to some new social order when peace came. I used to imagine an international party of ex-combatants, united by their common suffering, who would turn against the politicians and the profiteers in every country, and create a society based on respect for the individual human being. But no such party came into existence. The war ended in despair in Germany, in silly jubilation in England, and in an ineffective spirit of retribution in France. The societies of ex-combatants that were formed in England devoted themselves either to jingo heartiness or to the organization of charitable benefits. We left the war as we entered it: dazed, indifferent, incapable of any creative action. We had acquired only one new quality: exhaustion.

I shall relate in a later chapter the stages by which I re-adapted myself to civilian life. Here I only wish to describe the immediate reaction and disillusionment. My political ideas had continued to develop during the war. I published articles on syndicalism and guild socialism in 1917 and 1918. But the political situation of 1919 offered no basis for allegiance or enthusiasm. The political parties were all in the hands of non-combatants, especially on the left; and deep within me was a feeling that I could not speak the language of such people, much less co-operate with them. It was not that I despised them: I even envied them. But between us was a dark screen of horror and violation: the knowledge of the reality of war. Across that screen I could not communicate. Nor could any of my friends who had had the same experience. We could only stand on one side, like exiles in a strange country. Twenty-six years have passed and we have experienced another war. My feelings have not changed. I have seen the men of another generation engaged in a similar enterprise. Perhaps they have been less confident that we were, less liable to be deceived; but we do not know - they were conscripts and as such their motives were enigmatic. And since it was not the same kind of war, its debris is heaped in a different shape.

    In the last days of our war its tragedy was to strike me with a sudden personal violence. My youngest brother, who had followed me into the Green Howards and served on the Italian Front, was killed in France by a stray bullet. I knew his battalion had been transferred to the French Front, but I had had no particular anxiety for him: he was so young and vivid that the mind could not entertain his image and death's together. I was back in England at the time, stationed at Middlesbrough among strangers; but perhaps I was grateful for this isolation. My grief was too violent to tolerate sympathy or consolation. I walked about blinded by tears. I remember that I fled from the Garrison Headquarters and sought the seclusion of a park in the town. For the first and only time I sought to expel my emotions by actualizing them in verse. It was a bleak October day, with the emblems of death and grief around me. The lines of an elegy came spontaneously to my mind:

> *The autumn leaves were angry*
> *And seemed to intend*
> *As they yellowly drooped in the languid air*
> *That life was a fragile mood and death*
> *A tremendous despair.*
>
> *The yellow leaves fell*
> *Like slow tears of gold on the face of the day:*
> *They fell to the earth with a faint, sad sigh.*
> *They sighed*
> *As the feet of the passers-by*
> *Crushed them into the moist, black soil,*
> *They sighed when the gentle wind*
> *Lifted them along the way.*
>
> *In the Park*
> *Old men swept the dead things in a heap to burn:*
> *Their last fragrance*
> *Floated about the naked trees.*
> *I thought as the women walked in the moist,*
>     *still day*
> *Wearing yellow chrysanthemums in their coats,*
> *A chrysanthemum was*
> *A pale, dishevelled emblem of death.*
>
> *The sun*
> *Was a silver pervasion across the sky:*

*From the sky*
*The dead leaves fell.*

There was a good deal more of the poem, angry and resentful, and vainly consolatory; but too raw for publication even at this distance of time. When the Armistice came, a month later, I had no feelings, except possibly of self-congratulation. By then I had been sent to dreary barracks on the outskirts of Canterbury. There were misty fields around us, and perhaps a pealing bell to celebrate our victory. But my heart was numb and my mind dismayed: I turned to the fields and walked away from all human contacts.

# INTRODUCTION TO A WAR DIARY

It is all too easy to dramatize the tragedy of the generation that came of age between 1914 and 1918, but the events have now become cool history, too cool and impersonal to have much relevance to the heat of battle. Here the process of getting familiar with the idea of death and nothingness can be observed in all its unconscious fatality. The mind in action was unformed, which meant it was all the more pitilessly exposed to those still unfamiliar ideas, like a snail that had not yet had time to grow a shell. It is curious to observe how difficult it was for such an exposed organ of sensibility to accommodate itself to the horror of a world for the first time committed to universal destruction. In their innocence the young men of that time thought that a monstrous mistake had been made – that by accident foul gases had been released which would drift away with the dawn of peace. They were impatient to make a new world once the old world had disappeared, but they were to be deceived. The war ended, they found themselves powerless. Exhausted by their sufferings, they submitted to the fiercer energies of the old men who had watched and waited from a safe distance. It was only ten years later with the publication of a German narrative that unexpectedly caught the attention of the whole world, that we could begin to speak again of our experiences. For most of us it was then too late.

In the years after the First World War the phrase 'a lost generation' was often on our lips. It was used emotively, of course, but it had a justification in awesome statistics. These, no doubt, are recorded in some official document, and can be looked up if the reader is curious. The diarist does not need them because he was, in the literal sense, a living witness of the slaughter, one of the few survivors. In the course of those four years he must have known, as sentient human beings, instinct with affections, aspirations and constructive purpose, several hundred young infantry men between the ages of eighteen and twenty-eight (older men, too, but this was the bracket that enclosed the great majority). Of those hundreds, at the end of the war, only a score or so were still alive. Of those that were killed, a fair proportion would have distinguished themselves in a peaceable world, as poets, painters, architects, scientists, philosophers and statesmen, or as good and simple men contributing to the health and happiness of their kind. The few that came through carried with them the knowledge of this loss; they stumbled into the post-war world like stragglers from a fallen outpost. It is to their credit that they rarely indulged in self-pity.

The Russian Revolution itself passes without a mention. It will be difficult for anyone born into a world of 'mass-communications' to realize how isolated a soldier could be, out there in Belgium or France. There were, of course, no broadcasts in those days, and no newspapers. Even a company officer would hardly know what was happening in the brigades to the right or left of him. Again the mountaineering simile is apt – each little group was isolated on some ridge of a high mountain. All it shared with the people on the other ridges of the mountain was the same storm.

When he left his isolated outpost and went back to England wounded or on leave the soldier found himself in an alien world. Siegried Sassoon was to give perfect expression to the feelings of anger and disgust which were then experienced. Even if, as in the case of Sassoon, the committed soldier was given the opportunity to stay in this 'bitter safety', he was finally driven back by feelings of remorse and by memories of those he had left 'in the mud':

> Why are you here with all your watches ended?
> From Ypres to Frise we sought you in the Line.'
> In bitter safety I awake, unfriended;
> And while the dawn begins with slashing rain
> I think of the Battalion in the mud.
> 'When are you going out to them again?
> Are they not still your brothers through our blood?

But all that comradeship was to vanish once the storm was over and the expeditionary forces (as they were significantly called) had returned to the platitudes of life – old soldiers might continue to meet at regimental reunions, battalion dinners; but they were now so many particularities, repelling each other by their different interests, different occupations, different places in the civilian hierarchy:

> The world was not renewed.
> There was no hope in the homestead and anger in the streets
> But the old world was restored and we returned
> To the dreary field and workshop, and the immemorial feud
> Of rich and poor. Our victory was our defeat,
> Power was retained where power had been misused
> And youth was left to sweep away

*The ashes that the fires had strewn beneath our feet.*

A few may for a moment have thought of forming a militant League of Ex-Combatants, of making this a political and revolutionary unit in the post-war scene. But they were quickly disillusioned. Some went back to the mines, some to the factories; a few tried to build a new life in countries not fouled by war. The majority – the diarist himself! – sought security and marriage and *bourgeois* comforts. In their new habitats they met, if ever they met again, as released animals who had returned to the jungle to take on the colours of a familiar environment. In spite of all those days of danger and of joy shared together, they were now strangers to each other, and would suddenly feel embarrassed and dismayed.

The Rest Camp – Boyelles.    August 2. 17.

# EXTRACTS FROM A WAR DIARY

28.i.15
Wareham, Dorset

I am in very uncongenial surroundings here.

Here Nietzsche and all divine heretics seem like a dream. The only compensation this life offers is that it brings me into direct contact with a class of men I wanted to know. They are a rough lot – mostly miners from Durham and Middlesbro'. And how different they are from the newspaper fiction. I don't think one per cent are here for spiritual motives. They are always grumbling about their food and pay and I must say I sympathize with them. Their food is disgusting. Most of them make allowances to their wives or mothers and so only get 3*s* a week pay. And these are men who have earned as much as 10*s* a day. The huts they live in are filthy. If we get away before an epidemic breaks out I shall be surprised. The attitude of the average officer to them is overbearing and supercilious. My position as one of these little, homage-receiving gods is very quixotic ...

Yesterday I had to take the names of men in my platoon who had weak eyes. There were several. It appears that the weakness is caused by staring at molten steel. One man had been blind for a week. Our civilization again!

24.vi.16[1]
Rugeley Camp, Staffordshire

I came to this dreadful place a week ago. The Medical Board gave me 'light duty' – but they don't understand the term here. We get up at 5.30 am and are at it till tea time and sometimes later. And all the time the same monotonous work – shouting oneself hoarse, trying to initiate remarkably dense recruits into the mysteries of 'forming fours', etc. I think I shall flee to the Front for a little peace at the earliest opportunity.

17.vii.16
Rugeley Camp, Staffordshire

I don't know whether you would be interested in this life of mine here. I don't think I am a sympathetic enough critic to give it the faintest tinge of glamour. I have hated the Army as such ever since the first day I knew it. And my hate grows rather than diminishes. Not that I am bitter about it. There is so much to amuse one in a quiet way. But to be the dumb pawn of any fool who happens to be your senior, is a position that anyone with any decent will of his own must needs find irksome. But of course there are compensations – above all that delightful camaraderie which, I suppose, is peculiar to a fighting Army, and which is something finer and manlier than anything I experienced either at School or College.

---

1 In the interval of fifteen months I had been to the Front. I was accidentally wounded in March, 1916, and returned to England for twelve months.

Numberrrrrr.... Ones

This place is made more hateful by the fact that we have for a Colonel one of the most unpleasant and objectionable men I ever met, or hope to meet. On the other hand I have made one or two good friends (of the transient kind).

I have a jolly little cubicle which I share with one of these friends. Naturally we make it cosy (as only *men* can). Carpets, curtains, easy chairs – everything complete. Our walls are adorned with the most select pictures (including some of my own futurist efforts, which cause no little sensation, and I must confess, a good deal of scorn and amusement). And of course I have my bookshelf: I had one in the trenches.

One great joy we have at this place. That is a really decent Band. And what is more, a first class string orchestra. Don't be afraid that I'm one of those terrible people who scorn everyone save Bach and the 'scientific' musicians. I think my musical appreciation is purely emotional. Beethoven, Mozart, Chopin – such are my favourites. Wagner I do *not* like, generally speaking.

By the way, I've been to France and back since I last wrote. I took a draft out to the Base and had a most enjoyable trip. We went via Folkestone and Boulogne. Then on to Etaples, which is the Base. Coming back I spent a day in Boulogne which I think is quite a decent place. It has old walls, like York, but prettier.

27.viii.16
Rugeley Camp, Stafford

I will start again – or rather finish. I've just returned from the Colonel's farewell tea party. You said some time ago, when I told you how everyone detested the man, that probably he had a nice side to his character. You were quite right. He has a charming wife, a nice house and garden and – a baby! And in these surroundings even he seemed charming.

21.xii.16
Rugeley

I have been told to expect orders from France very soon.

29.xii.16
Rugeley Camp

I am in a condition such as demands amusement as a cure: that is, I am an invalid – though not a despondent one. I have been struggling with the demon of bronchitis for more than a week (he was with me last Sunday and must have made me rather a dull fellow). The demon conquered in the end and we're now good bedfellows. Don't imagine that I desire or deserve a scrap of condolence – I rather look for envy: An excellent little servant to attend to my every need: a Scotch cook who, despite her scorn of my vegetarian proclivities - which I thought sickness might excuse – is otherwise ideal: a stove which, although it sometimes smokes out of the wrong end, is nevertheless nice and warm: an easy chair – a dressing-gown and Meredith at his best (in *One of our Conquerors*) –

and all this in my fashionably furnished 'studio'. Did I ever describe the latter? 15' x 12'. Floored with antique matting – Greek couch (some people call it a camp-bed) – my walls decorated with a series of Japanese prints, three charcoal sketches of Watteau's, two of Whistler's, three or four of my own productions (note the conceited company I keep), a shelf of books, an oak table, a writing table and a few photographs of friends. Add to this a tapestried dado of discarded coats (etc.) drooping in languorous attitudes around the room and you get a *tout ensemble* that makes an illness Elysium!

But war is a tragic paradox: it destroys that which it should preserve. To any right-minded person life is sacred: so that the question of war becomes a question of values: is such an ideal *which can be obtained only by war*, of more value than life? Modern war is largely actuated by economic aggression. And that 'ideal' can hardly be compared with life. But a war for justice, for liberty, he who loses his life in such a war shall find it.

14.ii.17
Brocton Camp, Stafford

My delightful military picnic here passes like lightning. Only another three weeks! And then France – I expect, and I think I hope.

9.iv.17
The Base

We did not depart for France until Saturday – the 7$^{th}$ – lucky number! The day was calm, etc, and so was the sea, and there was a terrific squash on board. And I announce with triumph. I WAS *NOT* SICK!!! The chemist said I shouldn't be. Nothing happened at Boulogne – I had a good feed and bought a book, and then we came on here. I've nothing but praise for the French railways: we did 15 miles in 4 hours, thus enabling us, when the mood took us, to get out and stretch our legs. We arrived at this Base about midnight. We saw brown tents extending for miles across the sand-dunes, and looking mighty romantic in the moonlight. But I didn't feel romantic: our valises could not be transported to our camp until the following morning: so we had to make the best of two 'doubtful' blankets and the bare boards. I tried to forget a year of luxurious ease (relative), but my hipbone kept reminding me of it.

When we awoke we found it was Easter Sunday. We spent the morning completing our equipment, getting such things as 'tin' helmets and gas-bags. We were told we might disappear between the hours of 3 pm and 9 pm. So disappear we did. Went down into the town – a place much favoured by artists before the war. I had been to the place twice before, and knew it fairly well, so I delegated unto myself the role of guide to my companions. I pointed out to them the curious absence of a sewerage system – they thought it was evident. We fled from it … and arrived by a beautiful walk through a wood at Paris Plage – an ultra-fashionable sea-side resort, much favoured by Americans in the days when they could get there. At present given over to the entertainment of officers – British, French and Portuguese – and Nurses. We had tea there. And so, back by tram, supper and to bed.

This morning we started training and we keep it up until we get posted to our units and then more travelling.

12.iv.17

Three weary days have passed, waiting rather impatiently for orders to proceed up to the line. I was inoculated this morning – and now umpteen million germs are disporting themselves in my blood, making me somewhat stiff – and cross.

But I really feel extraordinarily calm and happy – very different sensations from those that accompanied my former 'coming out'. Then I felt reckless with the rest – and rather bacchanalian. Didn't care a hang what happened. And, in a way, I don't care a hang this time, but it's a different way, a glad way. And it rather troubles my soul to know why? Because, as you may know, I'm not exactly a warrior by instinct – I don't glory in fighting for fighting's sake. Nor can I say that I'm wildly enthusiastic for 'the Cause'. Its ideals are a bit too commercial and imperialistic for my liking. And I don't really hate the Hun – the commonest inspiration among my comrades. I know there are a lot of nasty Huns – but what a lot of nasty Englishmen there are too. But I think my gladness may be akin to that Rupert Brooke expressed in one of his sonnets:

> *Now God be thanked who has match'd us with His hour,*
>   *And caught our youth, and wakened us from sleeping,*
> *With hand made sure, clear eye, and sharpen'd power,*
>   *To turn, as swimmers into cleanness leaping,*
> *Glad from a world grown old and cold and weary,*
>   *Leave the sick hearts that honour could not move,*
> *And half-men, and their dirty songs and dreary,*
>   *And all the little emptiness of love.*

Though I must say I'm not yet so 'fed up' with the world as the sonnet implies. I haven't yet proved 'the little emptiness of love'. The half-men I still have with me in goodly numbers. And I've still faith that there are hearts that can be moved by honour and ideals. But England of these last few years has been rather cold and weary, and one finds little left standing amid the wreckage of one's hopes. So one is glad to leap into the clean sea of danger and self sacrifice. But don't think that I'm laying claim to a halo. I don't want to die for my king and country. If I do die, it's for the salvation of my own soul, cleansing it of all its little egotisms by one last supreme egotistic act.

All this is rather melodramatic; and forgive me if it is morbid. It is only a mood and has more to do with inoculation than anything else. I simply must not write any more until I'm properly 'sterilized'.

16.iv.17

*Le diable est mort* – long ago. In fact, God's in his heaven, all's right with the world, and I'm feeling quite

Browningesque. I haven't got my movement orders yet, but I've been posted to the 10th Battn., so my address will be: 10th Yorkshire Regt., BEF, France.

I would rather have gone to my old battn. – the 7th – but I have two or three friends in the 10th, so I mustn't grumble.

28.iv.17

I arrived at my battalion last night, after wandering over the face of France for three days. The first day we trained: the next two we had to march: and 'march' doesn't mean a pleasant country stroll – it means stumbling along rocky roads, getting pushed into gutters by passing lorries, one's back breaking with a heavy pack.

On the second day's march, the scenery began to be interesting, but not exactly inspiring. Before long we came to the old line of trenches, occupied about a month ago. Thereafter the country we passed thro' had, until recently, been in the hands of the Boche. I'm not going to attempt to describe the desolation of it: Philip Gibbs & Co do that well enough: it is enough to say that it is simply flattened, every feature (trees, houses, everything) just pulverised.

From this you will guess that I am in the thick of the new fighting. We are not in the trenches, but expect to go up sooner or later. But it is intensely interesting: no fear of getting bored here. The guns are going all day and night. This morning, very early, we were wakened by a furious strafe. You know what ordinary thunder is like: imagine that continuous for a couple of hours and yourself not listening to it, but inside the heart of it: that's something like it. And then the air is one continuous quiver of gun-flashes: and there's a battery just behind us which just gives the final touch to the entertainment: every few minutes it goes off with such a bang!-bang! that one fairly jumps out of one's skin.

I like my new battalion very well on first impressions: there are three other officers in my company, and they are all very decent fellows: the Captain exceptionally so. So I expect I shall be quite happy. We are all optimists out here. We've got the Boche absolutely cowed, and our men are splendid. There are big events pending – and if they go as we expect the war will be over in no time. With a bit of ordinary luck I'll see you sometime these summer holidays.

8.v.17

I think it's about ten days since I wrote to you last. Then I had just joined my battalion and we were basking indolent in the sun. But they didn't leave us basking long. On the Sunday we moved nearer the line and bivouacked for two nights. Then we moved up into the front line. Things have changed a lot in the last twelve months. Trenches as I knew them are a thing of the past. This time I found myself with my platoon in an isolated outpost in front of the Hindenburg line. We were 'dug in' in a narrow trench, with no dug-outs or any of the conveniences of a permanent trench. During the day we had nothing to do save endure with what patience we could muster the continuous bombardment.

But at night I had to go out on patrol with an NCO to examine the enemy's wire to see the damage our artillery had done to it during the day. Of all the ghastly jobs! It was bright moonlight every night. The enemy is at least 500 yards away. We walk the first 300 yards or so. Then we crawl, from shell-hole to shell-hole, until we dare go no further. It is difficult to say where prudence ends and fear begins. We stay there for about half an hour listening and peering into the dark, occasionally lit up by the enemy's rockets. Everywhere around us are indefinite shadows which every now and then our imagination endows with evil life.

We were in that outpost five days, with never a wash, living on tinned food, biscuits and drinking tea that tasted like a mixture of ink and petrol. Then we came out into the reserve trench, a mile behind. And, thank God, a wash. But still I haven't had my clothes off for 9 days and see no immediate prospect of getting them off. And never a BATH since 20 days ago, I , to whom a bath is a daily shrine, in which I do not merely tepidly glow, but ecstatically exult. I feel the dirtiest of sinners.

Here we are in the midst of an immense battle, accounts of which you will see in the papers. Any day we may have to go up and make an attack: otherwise our existence is lazy, and consists of eating, sleeping and enduring shellfire. Two officers who came out with me, have already been wounded, so I guess I shan't be long.

9.v.17

One thing troubles me: that you don't understand why I am out here: I thought I had made that clear. I've no doubt about my position. If I were free today, I'm almost sure I should be compelled by every impulse within me to join this adventure. For I regard it as an adventure and it is as an adventure that it appeals to me. I'll fight for Socialism when the day comes, and fight all the better for being an 'old soldier'. It is my desire to disassociate myself from the red, white and blue patriot that makes me 'growl'. Why a person like myself *can* fight with a good heart in a war like this, I have tried to express in the enclosed unfinished article. I have one or two good friends who are active conscientious objectors (one of them in prison) and they fail to see why I should be so militant in what they regard as an extraneous cause. I've always *felt* that I was in the right and now I am trying to express my feelings.

11.vi.17

There's a pleasant rumour today that we are going back a mile or two nearer civilization. But we know that it is only the calm before the storm. Nevertheless there's the alluring prospect of a primitive bath.

Picture us, with the help of the enclosed smudge, in our hovel – a place you wouldn't put a hen into in England. We are dirty but cheerful. Our Captain plays the flute, like any pagan from Arcady. The other fellow who completes our little company, and I, grovel on our only couch – Mother Earth. We are clothed in strange array – Tommy's clothes – 'gladrags', a gas respirator like a small chemical laboratory, and steel helmets – the only poetic thing in the British Army, for they are primeval in design and effect, like iron mushrooms. We do growl occasionally – at the guns that keep us awake, at the petrol that flavours everything we drink, but generally we are always merry and bright. C. ascribes this fact to the absence of women within a radius of at least 10 miles, and I do not vigorously dispute his cynicism.

22.v.17

Spring we do have here, but in an abortive sort of way. The felled trees bloom, but for the last time, and forget-me-nots spring up among the ruins. But everything is sad, and our few flowers are like wreaths among so much desolation.

The lull I told you of is lasting longer than we expected and we have now been in rest ten days. It is significant that during this time I have never been tempted to write to you – our present existence is rather passive and unimpressive. We spent most of the first week cleaning – skins and clothes. We are up early, drilling, etc, until noon, and then the rest of the day is left to our own devices, which mostly take the form of football, riding, eating, reading and various shooting competitions. Last night we had a pierrot party to entertain us – *al fresco*. But any day – any hour – we expect sudden orders to go back into the thick of it. And none of us really cares how soon these orders come, for the sooner our fate is settled the better, we argue.

15.vi.17

My present location is not too bad. We are now in the third week of our period in the line. (We went in shortly after my last letter to you.) We had seven days in the trenches and rather terrible days they were. But you can have no desire for me to 'paint the horrors'. I could do so but let the one word 'fetid' express the very essence of our experiences. It would be a nightmare to any individual. But we create among ourselves a wonderful comradeship which I think would overcome any horror or hardship. It is this comradeship alone which makes the Army tolerable to me. To create a bond between yourself and a body of men and a bond that will hold at the critical moment, that is work worthy of any man and when done an achievement to be proud of.

Incidentally my 'world-view' changes some of its horizons. I begin to appreciate, to an undreamt of extent, the 'simple soul'. He is the only man you can put your money on in a tight corner. Bombast and swank carry a man nowhere out here. In England they are everything. Nor is the intellect not a few of us used to be so proud of of much avail. It's a pallid thing in the presence of a stout heart. Which reminds me of one psychological 'case' which interest me here: to what extent does a decent philosophy of life help you in facing death? In other words: Is fear a mental or a physical phenomenon? There are cases of physical fear – 'nerves' 'shell-shock', etc. There are also certainly cases of physical courage – men who don't care a damn for anything – and there are men who have never thought a single moment on life and death or any 'problem'. And there are, I think, men who funk because they haven't the strength of will or decency of thought to do otherwise. These are fairly simple cases and to me obvious in daily experience. But I would like to think there was still another class (and I one of them) whose capacity for not caring a damn arose not merely from a physical incapacity for feeling fear, but rather from a *mental* outlook on life and death sanely balanced and fearlessly followed. But perhaps I idealize. At any rate, I moralize.

After seven days in the line we were a few days in Brigade reserve, which is fairly 'cushy'. Now we are up again, not actually in the trenches but in a sunken road, from which we daily or nightly sally forth to *dig* in or about the front line. But we do get a decent sleep fairly regularly and don't grumble. And there is the prospect of another 'rest' not far away.

This morning three prisoners were brought into the Cage which is just a few yards away. I was present at the examination by the Intelligence Officer and an interesting hour or two I spent. They were caught by a patrol last night. The most remarkable thing about these (and all the Boche we see) is their comparative cleanliness. And they always have greatcoats on whenever they are caught. And the weather is simply 'sweltering'. One of the prisoners was a very intelligent specimen and gave us a lot of valuable information. Another was a mere kid – said he was twenty but looked seventeen – and was so tremulous that he too, unwittingly, but perhaps not unwillingly, told us many things we wanted to know. I think we rather envied them: no doubt they have a rough time before them: but their 'fate' has arrived.

17.vi.17

I've been chosen for a death or glory job soon to come off. I am very glad – glad in the first place because it gives me the first chance I've had of doing something – glad in the second place because it means that others recognize that I'm of the clan that don't care a damn for anything.

All the same I intend to 'come through' as full of life as anything.

1.viii.17

Well, the 'stunt' is over, so now I can tell you something about it. I, along with another officer, was detailed to get as many volunteers as we could from our company and, on a certain dark and dirty night, to raid the enemy's trenches, kill as many as possible and bring back at least one prisoner for identification purposes. Out of a possible 60 we got 47 volunteers ... That was a jolly good start. We had about a fortnight to make our plans and rehearse. This we set about with enthusiasm – everybody was keen. Our plans were made with all the low villainous cunning we were capable of. When the battalion went into the front line we were left behind to train and take things easy. We two officers had to do a good amount of patrolling and observation. We had to discover the weak points in the enemy's wire, the best routes thither and as much of the enemy's habits as we could ... This went on until the fateful night arrived. Picture us about midnight: our faces were blackened with burnt cork, everything that might rattle was taken off or tied up. We armed ourselves with daggers and bombs and various murderous devices to blow up the enemy's wire and dugouts – and, of course, our rifles or revolvers. The raid was to be a stealth raid and depended for its success on surprise effect. So out thro' our own wire we crept – our hearts thumping but our wills determined. We had 540 yards to traverse to the objective. The first half were simple enough. Then we began to crouch and then to crawl – about a yard a minute. Suddenly, about 150 yards from the German trenches, we saw and heard men approaching us. We were following one another in Indian file. They seemed scattered to the right and left as far as we could see. In a moment all our carefully prepared plans were thrown to the winds. New plans had to be made on the spur of the moment. Our position was tactically very weak. My fellow officer began to crawl carefully back to reorganize the men into a defensive position, leaving me in front to deal with the situation if necessary. I could now see what was happening. The Huns were coming out to wire (had already started as a matter of fact) and were sending out a strong covering party to protect the wirers from surprise. This party halted and took up a line in shell-holes about twenty yards from us. Then some of them began to come forward to reconnoitre. We lay still, looking as much like clods of earth as we possibly could. Two Boche were getting very near me. I thought we had better surprise them before they saw us. So up I get and run to them pointing my revolver and shouting 'Haende hoch' (hands up), followed by my trusty sergeant and others. Perhaps the Boche didn't understand my newly acquired German. At any rate they fired on me – and missed. I replied with my revolver and my sergeant with his gun. One was hit and shrieked out. Then I was on the other fellow who was now properly scared and fell flat in a shell-hole. 'Je suis officier!' he cried in French. By this time there was a general fight going on, fire being opened on all sides. In a minute or two the guns were on and for five minutes it was inferno. The real object of the raid was achieved – a prisoner and a valuable one at that had been captured. So I began to make my way back with him whilst the other officer organized covering fire. In another five minutes we were back in our own trenches, and, all things considered, very glad to get there. Our casualties were only one missing and two slightly wounded. We must have inflicted twenty on the enemy, for, besides our rifle fire and bombs, we drove him back into a barrage put up by our trench mortars.

I took the prisoner along to Headquarters. He spoke a little French, so on the way we carried on a broken conversation. He told me his name, age, that he was married and where he came from. When we got to HQ there was an officer who spoke German and then the prisoner began to talk twenty to the dozen. We gave him a drink, cigarette, etc. He turned out to be an ex-schoolmaster of some sort and a very intelligent fellow. We got any amount of useful information from him. He was very interesting on things in general. Does not think we shall ever win this war, but neither will they. Says the new man, Michaelis, is a people's man and will gradually democratize the German government. But the Kaiser is still the people's hero and we must not expect the German nation to consent to his dethronement in the terms of peace. He says there is no chance of a revolution in Germany. Did not think much of the French, but was almost enthusiastic in his praise of the English. Said it was a mistaken idea to think the Germans hated the English. That was only an idea propagated by the German militarists and our own Press. We were of the same racial stock – should be allies - not enemies – etc, etc.

He himself won the Iron Cross at Verdun where he took 85 French prisoners.

We had to take him down to Brigade – an hour's walk. It was a beautiful early morning and everything was peaceful and the larks were singing. In our broken French we talked of music. He played both the violin and the piano and we found common enthusiasms in Beethoven and Chopin. He even admired Nietzsche and thenceforth we were sworn friends. He wrote his name and address in my pocket-book and I promised to visit him after the war if I ever came to Germany. By the time I handed him over to the authorities at the Brigade we were sorry to part with each other. And a few hours previously we had done our best to kill each other. *C'est la guerre* – and what a damnable irony of existence ... at any rate a curious revelation of our common humanity.

22.vii.17

Yesterday I had a day in Amiens. The Army is becoming quite a benevolent old gentleman, arranging little joy-rides for us when we are in reserve. This time it was too far for a bus and we had to put up with a French train. It meant getting up at 5 am, and walking 2½ miles to the station, but that was done willingly enough. Then rather a weary journey lasting 2½ hours. We passed through the valley of the Somme – past Albert, with its leaning Virgin – (when it falls, according to the superstition of Tommy, the war ends. – I would like to have charge of a German battery for a few hours) – finally arriving in Amiens, about 9.30 in time for breakfast – so we thought. Then we made a discovery: In civilized France they have food regulations. You may not eat in a public restaurant before 11 am. Not even a cup of coffee could we get. So we raided a *pâtisserie* and ate cream cakes over the counter. Thus refreshed, we wandered around the city. Naturally we made for the Cathedral and spent an hour or so there. I can't go into ecstasies about it. It is fine, of course, especially the exterior. The front is really great – delicate and finely wrought without any sacrifice of massive nobility. But the body of the cathedral tails off miserably and has a mean slender spire out of harmony with the frontage. There are some fine flying bastions, or whatever they call them, which would make a finer 'vorticist' design. The interior is disappointing – neither austere nor beautiful. A service was in progress and a priest was delivering a remarkably dramatic sermon – all about poor little Belgium and the horrible Hun. Vergers walked up and down dressed in the gaudiest uniforms I've ever had the pleasure of seeing – and all alike as two peas – with mutton-chop whiskers like English butlers.

After the cathedral we did our shopping. I had to buy crockery for the Mess (being Mess President) and I did this in great style. Other 'necessaries' soon made our money go and we ourselves were soon aware of our stomachs. So then lunch – nothing unusual except peaches. After lunch more sightseeing. Amiens itself is like any other cathedral town except that it has more fine modern buildings – one of the best of the latter is the Musée de Picardie where we saw the famous mural decoration of Puvis de Chavannes and a bust by Rodin.

27.vii.17

We are in the line again now. It promises to be rather an interesting trip for me, but of this more later.

2.ix.17

We are now 'enjoying' a rest! That blessed word 'rest'. It has terrors for us almost equal to any the line can produce. It means constant scrubbing and polishing and an almost Bond Street atmosphere in the midst of some dirty old broken down village. And then a continual state of *qui vive*, for safety releases all kinds of horrors upon us: fellows with red hats and monocles who seldom molest us in our natural haunt. Then that figure familiar to all in England through Bairnsfather's sketches – Old Bill – has to be renovated, drilled and cursed until he somehow resembles his pre-war edition. No mean task this – only to be accomplished by the expense of much raucous voice and more patience. Then we've got in our Company forty odd recruits raw from England without the foggiest notion of war. *Then* Tommy takes it into his head to write letters to all his old pals and sweethearts long neglected, and so two or three weary subalterns have to wade through two or three hundred uninteresting letters every day. *Comme ci*: 'Dear old pal – Just a line hoping as how you are in the pink of condition as this leaves me at present. Well, old pal, we are out of the line just now in a ruined village. The beer is rotten. With good luck we shall be over the top in a week or two, which means a gold stripe in Blighty or a land-owner in

BILL TOWERS

France. Well, they say it's all for little Belgium, so cheer up, says I: but wait till I gets hold of little Belgium.

>From your old pal,
Bill.

And so on until they become anything but funny. But there are compensations. After tea we are generally left to our own devices. Sometimes Col and I will get horses and away for a ride. Sometimes I think a ride together beats a walk. There is more exhilaration. A sense of communion, not only between yourselves, but also between you and your horse. Here and there a cross-country track gives us the chance of a gallop and away we go! We get back just before dark, glowing with the exercise and hearts as happy as can be. Again, the nights this last week have been divine – cold moonlight. Washed in this silver light this land loses all its look of desolation. The whitewashed houses make the village streets look almost painfully English. The fields are all misty and the shadowy trees mysterious. In many places we have just reaped a harvest sown by the Germans in spring. And what scene can compare to a harvest-field by moonlight? Yellow stooks pitched like the tents of an army: perhaps a dark wood flanking one side of the picture: and the clumsiest farm-stead you could possibly desire somewhere in the misty perspective. Such joys as these make us forget entirely the horrors none of us desires to remember. Things even seem 'worthwhile'.

5.ix.17 – very pm

Life is 'intense' nowadays – never a minute to one's self, as they say. On the 3rd Col and I went to Amiens together for the day. Up at 5 am and a glorious ride to the nearest station, with the day scarce dawned. We had a happy school-boy sort of day, buying things and eating enormous meals. You would laugh at the tremendous importance 'food' assumes out here. We romped all day till we were wearied out – and then a four hours' journey in a crowded train! And we didn't get corner seats, and it was a third-class carriage, which, in this benighted land, isn't much better than a cattle-truck. We tried to prop each other up and go to sleep like Babes in the Wood, but not with much success. But joy revived in the ride back in the moonlight, and finally we agreed that it was 'the end of a perfect day'.

Just now in from another moonlight ramble – and as happy as a lark.

9.ix.17

We move soon to another part for a big show.

I was 'dished-out' with a ribbon this am by the Major-General. Terrible ordeal in front of the Brigade. But it's over now.

7.x.17

When I arrived behind the line I found that the Battalion were in the thick of the fight. I had to stay behind until they came out, along with two others who had straggled in. All such stragglers for all the Brigade are billeted together – about 15 of us. We have a large mess-hut wherein some passing genius has built a wide open old-English fireplace of bricks. Fuel in plenty appears miraculously, so, as the weather is vile and tempestuous we build the fire high and sit round in a circle. We are rather quiet, not knowing what has happened to our friends. Vague rumours come down to us every now and then. So-and-so is killed, so-and-so is wounded. The ----- have only two officers left out of the twenty that went in to action. I hear that Col is wounded, but still 'carrying on'. That sounds like him. Later someone comes down with shell-shock. He seems distracted and does not know anything definite. Some he has seen killed, others wounded. A few grim details he can give us. The attack was a great success – all objectives taken and so on. But for all we want to know we shall have to wait until they come out. The latest rumour says that is tomorrow and that we are going back to reorganize. We can only hope so.

I feel a little ashamed of having escaped it all. There is always a regret in not having shared dangers with friends. Perhaps one is jealous of their experiences. Only I have some consolation.

9.x.17

Yesterday I was detailed to go to a village about 30 miles behind and find billets for the battalion who were coming out of the line for a rest. I took four NCOs with me and boarded a bus for the benighted little place I am now in. Consists of one church, about twenty estaminets, and, of all things on earth, a corset factory! I have spent part of yesterday and all today doing my Sunday best in French with people who talk a weird half-Flemish lingo that is to French about what Cockney is to good broad Yorkshire. The majority of them are rather suspicious and hostile and I've had a terrible time with them. But the result is fairly satisfactory and now I am waiting for the battalion to come in – sometime in the 'small hours'.

Last night I found a jolly old dame, who provided me with a truly magnificent 'chambre', all curtains and crucifixes. She was an admirer of 'les braves anglais' and treated me to innumerable cups of coffee and talked away far into the night. As she grew tired she became sentimental, finally weeping over '*tous les morts, francais, anglais* et boches'. Then she went to sleep in her chair and I retired to the magnificent 'chambre'. Today I met the priest, a big man in long flowing black robes and a horribly dirty face. He plays weird music on a cracked piano and is awfully proud of a WC he has – 'the only one in the village'. Another kind old man insisted on cutting me several bunches of grapes that were growing along the roof of his house. I went to see the 'maire' expecting to find a very important personage, especially as I was directed to the 'château'. I found the dirtiest man I've ever seen picking potatoes in a field! He didn't seem to know very much about anything and referred me to his secrétaire, who turned out to be the publican of 'The Cyclists' Rest'. He rummaged amongst a heap of 'sugar tickets' and grubby children and produced a list of householders and a plan of the village. After that we were fast friends and I got along swimmingly. But I still hae ma doots whether they'll all 'get in' or not. *Mais c'est la guerre*, as they all say.

10.x.17

They came in shortly after midnight, very weary and ready to drop down and sleep anywhere. It isn't three weeks since I left them, but it was like greeting long lost friends. Col is all right, only a scratch or two: but it will take time for him to throw off the gloom of their terrible experiences. It isn't only fancy that makes them seem to have aged five years or more. They have gone through what was probably the most intense shell fire since the war began. As a battalion we have been remarkably lucky – only one officer killed and not so many men as one would expect. A lot wounded, but most of them can be considered lucky. One or two of my special pals among the men have disappeared, especially a jolly little Irish boy who was worth a thousand for his cheerfulness. I don't know how long we shall be out at rest. I am afraid not long.

26.x.17

We have had a terrible time – the worst I have ever experienced (and I'm getting quite an old soldier now). Life has never seemed quite so cheap nor nature so mutilated. I won't paint the horrors to you. Some day I think I will, generally and for the public benefit. I was thoroughly 'fed up' with the attitude of most of the people I met on leave – especially the Londoners. They simply have no conception whatever of what war really is like and don't seem concerned about it at all. They are much more troubled about a few paltry air raids. They raise a sentimental scream about one or two babies killed when every day out here hundreds of the very finest manhood 'go west'. Of course, everyday events are apt to become rather monotonous ... but if the daily horror might accumulate we should have such a fund of revulsion as would make the world cry 'enough!' So sometimes I wonder if it is a sacred duty after all 'to paint the horrors'.

My military progress continues – strange to say. I am now commanding a company and may soon be a captain. I believe I have been rather conscientious since I came to this battalion - I don't know why – perhaps life is so much more enjoyable if one works hard. At any rate, I am satisfied. I thoroughly enjoy my despotism and a company commander is a terrible despot. He tries all his criminals and dispenses what he may consider justice, or sends them to a higher court (the Colonel): he gives promotion to all who serve him well; exacts obedience: directs his government - redresses all grievances. So imagine me, if you can, in the role. I am democratic so far as the Higher Powers permit. For example, I put it to the vote whether RUM should be issued last night or this morning - ie the rum: they don't care very much about the 'when' so long as it is reasonably often. I have got a fine lot of lads though they are fastly decreasing in numbers. 'Always merry and bright' - it's my aim to keep them so. And they are a gallant crew: we have more decorations in our company than in any other in the battalion. I got four Military Medals today out of seven for the battalion. And damn proud of it we all are.

My subalterns (notice the 'my' - sort of possessive pride) are quite a good lot and mostly my seniors in age - Gipsy Lee is almost old enough to be my father. Bevan is the youngest and a good friend. He is Devon born, lives in Wales and has sojourned a good while in Canada. Hence he is sturdy, frank and sensible. His nice eyes, hazel and liquid perhaps betray his inner nature. Sentimental, of course. He was, and still is, madly in love, but alas! the fickle maid has jilted him. But his heart is not broken nor his cheery outlook much affected.

Hart is a famous runner and like all competitive sportsmen, rather boastful. But he is a good fellow and runs our Mess in an ideal manner. He would make an excellent hotel manager. He, too, is very sentimental, and plays patience with a pack of photos of the fair one.

Gipsy Lee has just joined us and is still a mystery.
Martin is a young rake of the Cockney variety with a wonderful variety of oaths, yarns of a doubtful nature, and a stutter that does not prevent him talking all day long.

There you have a scandalous account of our society and I'm not really ashamed of being the author of it, for I know they do the same by me, and I don't mind.

14.xi.17

Today the post arrived just as Col and I were off for a ride. We read our letters - he had one of the right kind too - as we ambled along in the winter sunlight. Then we both laughed gladly and vowed we had never known such a perfect moment.

We are out of the line again, after another terrible week. We hope never to see this sector again. Expect to go back for a few weeks rest any day now. Then I will write to you. I feel too unsettled now - my present home a tent in an ocean of mud. I fear I was rather a dull fellow in my last letter. I'm going to give economics a rest.

I think I too have 'the glad consciousness' of returning to England soon. At any rate, some fine day.

19.xi.17

We are on the trek: for three days we have marched away from the northern horrors and still we march - for another two days. I am enjoying it all immensely - I suppose it is the reaction - and the weather is quite passable - ideal for our purpose - misty November days, with an occasional gleam. So contented are we that we don't mind much the fact that our long promised rest has been postponed a while - but only a short while.

This is where we touch the romantic fringe of war - for it is only a fringe, the romance. Now we have all the thrills of a sentimental journey - all the excitement of changing environment and of strange meetings. Our experiences vary: the first journey's end was rather disconcerting. Our billet was the almost inevitable farm-house: our men were safely and snugly packed into a hay loft; and we ourselves entered the house; and the dourest (I think that is the exact word) face imaginable greeted us. Our 'rooms' were good enough, though rather bare. But we were tired and hungry and would partake of the usual café and omelettes. But no: she would not make us anything. Would she let our cook use her stove? No. There was a stove in our rooms, so would she let us have some coal to cook with? Again a gruff refusal. 'Madame no bon', is the frank opinion of Towers (my servant). So we are left to our own devices. I forgot to mention that we had bought some fish as we passed through a town. 'You *must* cook that fish, or go and drown yourselves' were our final orders to the domestic staff. Thus having delivered ourselves we went and sat, glum as moulting hens, in our bleak bedroom. After a while we heard the chopping and cracking of wood, then the frizzling of a frying-pan and finally the fish appeared and jolly good it was.

The epilogue was a little account delivered to me in the early morning before we set out:

*5 hen perches ... 1 fr. 50.*

I blinked amazedly for a few moments and then I remembered the cracking and chopping of wood!

The next journey's end was very different. The NCO who had gone in advance, on our arrival, pointed out to me an innocent enough looking house and said, 'That's your mess.' I entered boldly enough, only to gasp and fall back on to the toes of whoever was behind me. Seated round a table, enjoying a meal of some sort, were at least six beaming maidens. They all shouted out 'Entrez!' So I thought I had better take my hat off and make another advance. 'Mess?' I weakly inquired. 'Là!' they pointed. And somehow I circumnavigated them and entered the next room, followed by my flabbergasted friends. Again we were tired and hungry, so again we asked (this time more humbly) for café and omelettes. Nothing could have pleased the old lady better (there was *one* old lady) and we had a delightful meal on the table in no time. This finished, and our morale recovered, we ventured back into the kitchen, where a gramophone was playing selections of English music, and, perhaps more inviting still, a French stove was roaring away and dispelling the chill of the November twilight. Chairs were pushed forward and we *had* to accept: and so a very pleasant hour or so ... Col came in then and we decided to go forth in quest of adventures to the fairly big town that was only a mile or so away. I was loath to leave that friendly kitchen, but Col was keen, so off we went, with another fellow (Hart - the runner.) We arrived there 5.30 pm. Went to order dinner at an hotel: saw an advertisement of *the* Pierrots: dashed off there and heard the best concert you can imagine. It was a Sunday, so the programme was perhaps more select than usual. At any rate, a violin soloist who seemed perfection. (Fancy, one week in the horrors I can't describe and the next listening to Chopin perfectly rendered). There were other things on the programme, all delightful, even if sentimental ... Then dinner, rather ordinary and back to bed by 10 pm ... Up again at 6 am and the trek resumed. And here I am in another hospitable billet, but no chorus of fair maidens, but an equally jolly old man, who has lit a stove in the room for us, and provided us with all he can - *even clean white sheets* - and that is heaven, or will be in an hour or so.

10.i.18

We are midway through a long weary tour of trench duty. We do four days in the line and then four in support and four in reserve - and this sometimes for more than a month. The four in reserve are the only ones during which it is possible to be civilized - to wash and change and write letters. As a Company commander I get a much easier time in the line - no long dreadful night-watches. I manage to get a little reading done. I also managed to write a short article and send it on to the *New Age*. I don't really expect them to accept it, as it is very much against their point of view. I called it 'Our Point of View' and my chief points were:

(a) That the means of war had become more portentous than the aim - ie that the game is not worth the candle.
(b) That this had been realized by the fighting soldier and on that account there has been, out here, an immense growth of pacifist opinion.

Of course, it might offend the Censor. But it is the truth. I know my men and the sincerity of their opinions. They know the impossibility of a knock-out blow and don't quite see the use of another long year of agony. We could make terms now that would clear the way for the future. If, after all that Europe has endured, her people can't realize their most intense ideal (Good-will) - then Humanity should be despaired of - should regard self-extinction as their only salvation. But I for one have faith, and faith born in the experience of war.

9.iii.18

It is June here. For three days there hasn't been a cloud in the sky and the larks have been singing all day long. And though we are actually in line, we find it hard to realize that there is a war on. Things are unearthly quiet. I am writing this out in the sun, and the scene round me is a wide amphitheatre about 600 yards in diameter, an old sandy quarry. It looks great in the early sun - a rich golden brown, but as the sun gets higher it turns yellower. Our dugouts are deep down in the sides of the quarry and quite comfortable with beds and tables. We keep a cat - a beautiful brown and white one, very clean and full of play and a foot-warmer by night. Yesterday I was down in the dugout all by myself and a big setter dog flopped in from heaven only knows where. The floor of the dugout is partly boarded and partly bare sand. Without taking the slightest notice of me he flopped down on the boards and proceeded to go to sleep. About ten minutes later, he got up and went over to the unboarded part of the dugout and there he clawed the sand until he made a round basin. This he found more comfortable and I thought he had finally settled. But soon after, his conscience must have pricked him, for he got up and came to me and was most affectionate, trying to lick my face and rubbing his snout against me. And all this without a word of invitation! So I concluded that it was another case of the Wonders of Instinct. When we had sweethearted long enough he went under the table - and there he got a shock for Pussy had taken up position under there. So many growls on the part of Pussy and whines and whimpers on the part of the dog. Eventually he disappeared and I've never seen him since. Pussy is much happier though.

17.iii.18

The great days are still with us. I went a walk this evening with Col to the top of a small hill that commands most of this flat country. The sun was just in his last glory and there was a slight mist on the ground. Westward this mist fused with the mellow sunlight and the land seemed to be covered with a thick golden dust. It hung about the distant trees like golden sow, and like snow, soon melted away, but not without a last transient flare of colour. I sat on the hill and watched it till it was all cold and colourless, and Col asking me if I had finished 'dreaming'.

1.iv.18

'It's lovely by the seaside' and that is where I am.

I alway feared that the beautiful peace I was telling you about was rather ominous. Suddenly one morning early (the 21st) it turned to a raging hell. What has happened since then I shall never get you told about until I have written a book about it. At present you must be satisfied with very bare facts.

We were rushed up to the line in the early hours of morning and from then and for six days and nights we were fighting as I never dreamt I would fight - without sleep - often without food and all the time besieged by hordes of the Boche. The Colonel was wounded during the second day and I had to take command of the battalion. We were surrounded in our original position and had to fight our way through. We took up position after position, always to be surrounded. On the whole the men were splendid and there were many fine cases of heroism. But our casualties were very heavy and we who have come through may thank our lucky stars eternally.

I couldn't let you have word before. Things like the post 'go to pot' in an affair like this. But I am all right now. I was a bit of a scarecrow at the end of it, but now we have been withdrawn to a beautiful quiet place near the sea, with nothing much else to do save sleep and eat.

Colin missed the first four days and I was glad of it (though he wasn't). We are sharing a billet here and are happier than ever. It is wonderful how happy you do feel when you find peace once more and yourself alive to enjoy it. I think the experiences of the last ten days have had rather a deep effect on me. I'll talk to you more about it when I'm more collected. I saw humanity very naked and life both precious and pitiful. By chance as I went out that morning of the 21st I slipped a book into my pocket. It was *Walden*. I didn't get a chance of looking at it the first six days, but in my wandering since I have read it and found much comfort there. In a very different way - the very opposite way - old Thoreau got to the naked reality of life and came to the same conclusions. It all drives me to an individualism, an anarchy which it is for each of us to realize. But more of this when I've thought more.

18.iv.18

Meanwhile - talking of the adventurous and strenuous life - I lead it. We have had a ten days' trip in our new sector, which isn't much of a change from the last, except in scenery. But it is a life that has little spiritual beauty in it, so hardly comes up to the demand of Thoreau & Co.

28.iv.18

I'm afraid the days of long letters are over for a while. Of course we have become involved in the fighting again and our life is terribly strenuous. We are all weary and almost broken-hearted. But we manage to keep up an appearance of unconcern. But it needs a strong will. I'm afraid Colin is affected: he is no longer the gay heart he used to be and even I have to infuse some spirit into him - a circumstance I should never have thought would come about - rather the other way round from my own idea of our respective temperaments.

Forgive me for writing in this gloomy mood. But nowadays to be false to the reality would choke me. I don't want you to think we are unhappy - we have comradeship in our troubles and that makes all the difference.

9.v.18

Our precious Colin is missing. We have been through hell for the second time in seven weeks and once again been cruelly smashed. Col was in the front line with his company. They were gassed and barraged with heavies for about four hours and then surrounded from all sides by the Boche. All day we had no news of them but in the evening we counter-attacked and took several prisoners - among them an officer who spoke very good English and was a fairly intelligent specimen. I questioned him about the morning's happenings and he said that a good few prisoners had been taken, among them a captain. Now Col was the only captain in the front line, so I feel pretty confident that it was he. Besides, the prisoner said that he had gold stars on his shoulder-straps, was very young and fair - all of which points to Colin. So I feel fairly happy about him. He, at any rate, is out of it and with ordinary luck should come through all right. I am the unfortunate one: I am robbed of my best friend in circumstances which make such a friend as Col half one's life. But for his sake I am glad.

How sick I am of the whole business. Most of the prisoners we took were boys under twenty. Apart from uniforms, German and English are as like as two peas: beautiful fresh children. And they are massacred in inconceivable torment. This is the irony of this war: individually we are the one as good as the other: you can't hate these innocent children simply because they dress in grey uniforms. And they are all magnificently brave, English and German alike. But simply because we are united into a callous inhuman association called a State, and because a State is ruled by politicians whose aim (and under the circumstances their duty) is to support and maintain the life and sovereignty of this monster, life and hope are denied and sacrificed. And look at their values. On the one hand national well-being and vanity, commercial expansion, power: on the other love, joy, hope - and all that makes life worth living - all that persuades one to consent to live among so much that is barbarous and negative. So perhaps you will begin to see the connection between 'the German push, Thoreau and anarchy'. And perhaps you will get 'a glimpse of how, in my hear of hearts, I regard my whole connection with the Army and its work'. I could make my connection with it something of a success *if I had the will*. *Without* the will I have not done so badly. I like its manliness, the courage it demands, the fellowship it gives. These are infinitely precious things. But I hate the machine - the thing as a whole and its duty (to kill), its very existence. My will is to destroy it and my energies must be devoted to that end. Is this the glimpse you wanted?

Colin's fate rather alters my outlook. Now I don't think I should hesitate to take the Staff job - it is no use making a martyr of one's self and clinging to this worst of existences in the Army. The Army does not take account of martyrdom and besides, I've been a martyr long enough to satisfy even my vanity. One the other hand the Staff job is a very uncertain one. In the meanwhile the certainty of flying may come. What then? I don't funk it by any means - I rather hanker after its 'romance'. On the other hand (the 'hands' are getting rather confusing, but never mind), to start flying now is to revolutionize my Army life to an unknown extent. That would have been all right with Col. But alone? And besides, the others in the battalion - old 'Pick' especially, ridicule the idea of me 'leaving them in the lurch'. To go to the Staff is a natural step - they would be 'proud' of me there. But to go to the Flying Corps is to desert them, to take an unnatural step. But in a family where 'desertions' are so often forced, a voluntary 'desertion' does not matter so much. I rather think I shall settle this muddle of 'to be or not to be' by accepting the first fate that comes my way: and if it is flying I shall fly.

17.v.18

I don't quite know where I left off in my last letter. So much has happened since then. We have wandered down to a new sector and have become practically a new battalion in all but name and I've been rather overwhelmed with work. But suffice it to say that I am now trying to do the almost impossible, which in this case is to lie my full length on the grass and write a letter. It is so hot that it is cruelty to move. But the grass is the lawn of a deserted garden, green and shady, with a few restful narcissi (almost my favourite flower, I think) to delight my eyes, birds 'cheeping' and only the drone of an aeroplane to remind one that war is our existence. Perhaps the quiet is a little too reminiscent of those happy days before St. Quentin to be altogether a joy. But still it is a blessed balm to our weary souls.

19.v.18

The loss of Colin drives me more than ever to the companionship of books. So you must not grumble if they overwhelm my letters. Apart from just a slight uneasiness, which will disappear when I hear definitely that he is safe, I cannot but feel quietly satisfied with his fate. The strain was killing his spirit, and in the comparative calm of a prisoner's life he would recover his buoyancy and will.

By now it is night outside - beautifully starlit. But there is a German aeroplane somewhere in the sky with evil intent and I have had to close the shutters to hide my light and to divide me from the beauties outside. You see how fugitive our peacefulness is!

**2.6.18** *[sic]*

We have had eight days in the line - beautifully peaceful. We are not, I am glad to say, involved in the latest débâcle.

**8.iv.18**

Colin is all right. His Elsie wrote to tell me that they had had a cable to say he was a prisoner and well. That's a great relief - to know for certain. I had persuaded myself to be very sure - but - war is war.

I'm very busy nowadays - but all very dull. I should say that being an Adjutant out here is worse than being the Managing Director and Secretary (rolled into one) of a firm of 1,000 employees in business. And I don't profess to be anything like a business man.

**14.vi.18**

The transfer has come through.[2] I ought to be in England by the 19th. I have to report there (London) - endure a medical board and then I hope get leave.

---

2 To the Royal Flying Corps. I was rejected by the medical board.

9.vii.18

On Friday I got a wire ordering me to report to the 3rd Battn. at West Hartlepool *for duty*. Arrived here on Saturday: they have not heard anything about me from the War Office. I got 48 hours' leave and went to London for my kit and to Leeds for some more and back here last night. Still no orders about me. But the adjutant here thinks it means at least a long stay in England.

20.vii.18

This you can regard as good news or otherwise: The doctor here examined me and says there's nothing much the matter with me except general 'run-down'. So France may not be a too distant prospect.

31.x.18

10 am. Investiture. Really a boring affair. A long wait: marshalling and a wholesale atmosphere: musical comedy music to accompany (isn't there a Beethoven Eroica than might have been more appropriate in a more cultured land?) But I got the bauble and there is a little satisfaction in that.

10.xi.18

Today I have written to the War Office cancelling my application for a regular commission. The war, I am glad to say, is over - much to some people's disappointment. I have been fairly disgusted these last few weeks. I do not think the national temper is anything to be proud of. Christian sentiments being out of fashion or obsolete, I thought we might at any rate have exercised the Englishman's renowned sense of fair play - of not hitting a man when he is down, etc. No. That is another damned hypocrisy exposed. We only do that when it pays. At present it will pay most of us to leave Germany incapacitated for foreign trade, etc, for a century. League of Nations? 'Damned idealistic rot. Can't imagine why we let a dreamy bloke like Wilson dictate to us. What I say is: Give 'em a taste of what they gave Little Belgium. Burn their villages, stick their babies, rape their women. And now for a strong Army & Navy and keep the old flag flying.'

Do you realize that that is the way the average Englishman is talking just now? I'll soon be out of all this, by fair means or foul. At present I am gagged, bound hand and foot, mutely to listen to such rot. If it is not demoralizing, it is enough to drive me mad.

At present I am wondering by what conceivable chain of circumstance, of flattery, promise of ease, blindness to reality, I came seriously to consider staying in the Army.

14.xi.18

Everybody went mad the other day.* I felt hopelessly sober. I read Henry James's *Sacred Fount* to the accompaniment of the rejoicings - with a savage zest.

* Armistice Day

# THE RAID

It was early summer and the warm sun seemed to reanimate the desolate land. Before one of a group of huts a young subaltern was seated at a table. He was bareheaded and the sun played on the bright yellow strands of his hair. He played nervously with a match-stalk, splintering it with his fingernails, scraping it aimlessly about the table. The sun played on the white bleached wood of the twirling match-stalk and on the dark blistered polish of the table. Nervous fingers rolled the hard stalk between soft plastic flesh. At times everything was very still. The dreamer wandered. The shreds of the match-stalk seemed far away, brittle legs of birds, pattering on the hard brown table. The sun was buoyed in some kind of space, hard to conceive; where, too, the mind swayed in utter helplessness.

    Why had all the horror suddenly become potent? Lieutenant P___ had been in France four months now, and all the time, in some degree, his life had been threatened. He had been sick, sick all the time – but the hunted life had each day sunk into renewing sleep; and day had succeeded day, and somehow the faith had been born that the days would pass in such a succession until the long terror was ended. But the present eventuality had made a difference. He had been selected to lead a raid, along with me, and a volunteer party of about thirty men. This sudden actualization of the diffused terror of our existence had made a difference to my friend. I could divine it as he sat there in his restless abstraction.

I was lying within the hut, beneath the corrugated vault of iron. My body was listless, my mind content. I saw P\_\_\_\_, crumpled in his chair – his boots drawn under, his untidy puttees, his rounded shoulders and over-big flaxen head. I saw men walking about the grassy plot in front of us, and in the sky, an easier reach for my recumbent eyes, a lark, a dot, a lark that was always singing in this region at the time of our stay there. The lark, and the men walking very near on a horizon, were more real to me than the vague wonder about my fate in the raid. I was afraid, but more interested in P_____'s fear. I decided that he must in some way be imprisoned in his flesh – despite that mind, floating vacantly in the ether. He was an undersized but thickset man of about twenty-three. He had a pale fleshy face and china-blue eyes, a coarse voice and a tendency to blush. He had been a teacher. He had a mother and a sweetheart, and he spent a lot of time writing letters. He never got free from his home thoughts; he was still bound in some sort of personal dependence to these ties. His mind, at any rate, was not free to lead its own existence, or to create the conditions of its existence. I think that is why he was a coward.

For he was a coward, in the only concise sense that can be given to that word. A coward is not merely a man who feels fear. We all experience fear; it is a physical reaction to the unknown extent of danger. But it is only cowardice when it becomes a mental reaction – when the mind, reacting to the flesh, submits to the instincts of the flesh.

As the time appointed for the raid grew nearer, P\_\_\_\_\_'s manner began to change. We had always been thrown together a good deal: we were the only officers in the Company with tastes in common. But we were scarcely friends; there was something in his physical nature that repelled me. But now he began to make up to me more insistently. Presently the remainder of the battalion went into the trenches and we were left to rest and train for our enterprise. P_____ then grew more confidential and spoke often of his home affairs. He seemed afraid to be out of my presence. He began to confess to me; to bemoan his fate; to picture the odds against us – the utter unlikelihood that we should ever come out of this business alive.

    I asked him if he was afraid. He blushed and said: 'Yes, damnably.' He was obviously in an agony of mind, and then I began to have my own fear: that he would bitch the show and bring disgrace on us all. I put this to him. We had left camp and were on a visit to battalion headquarters, a mile or two behind the line. There was some sort of gun emplacement or old trench line into which we had climbed to look out over the sun-soaked plain: the larks were singing as always in the still clear sky. But P_____'s face looked aqueous and blotchy. His eyes were uneasy, reflecting all his anguish. After a while I asked him to make a clean breast of it all to the Colonel. But I saw that he would never do that. He just hung his head and looked stupid.

    When we reached the battalion I left P_____ outside and went into the Colonel's shanty or dugout. I told him about P_____ ; deliberately. He was immediately taken off the raid and S_____ , an elderly subaltern who had already taken part in a previous raid, was asked to take his place. This he did with a bad grace.

    P_____ was killed in a bombardment some months later. A night of confused darkness and sudden riot.

We greased our hands and faces and then blackened them with burnt cork so that they would not shine out in the dark night. We muffled our rifle slings and accoutrements so that no little noise should betray us. Then we made our way into the trenches to the point selected for our sally. A terrace such as is often found in French fields ran across no-man's-land, at right-angles to the trenches. It led to an elbow in the enemy's line, and the concerted plan was that at midnight exactly the artillery and trench mortars should isolate this elbow with a barrage of fire, whilst we penetrated into the trenches and secured some of the enemy, dead or alive. We raiders were to creep along the guiding line of the bank in Indian file until within thirty yards or so of the enemy's position, then to creep round into a compact line facing the trench: this movement to be achieved by midnight. Then, immediately the barrage fell, we were to rush forward and do our best.

It was agreed that I should head the Indian file, and that S_____ should bring up the rear. He was to prevent straggling and to see that the line swung round into position when I sent back the signal. The last thing we did before going out was to give each man a stiff dose of rum: then there were a few whispered farewells and a handshake or two. The night was moonless, but fair, and not quite pitch dark. You could distinguish a silhouette against the skyline. As soon as we passed our own wire entanglements we got down on our bellies and began to crawl. I had already explored the ground in two or three special night patrols, and had no difficulty in finding the bank and getting the right direction. I advanced a step at a time, the sergeant close behind me.

I felt that I ought not to neglect a single aspect of that slow advance to the enemy's lines, for in those few minutes I experienced a prolonged state of consciousness during which I hung over a pit of fear, weighted down by a long and vivid anticipation of its nature, and now brought to the last tension by this silent agony of deliberate approach. Fear is more powerful in silence and loneliness, for then the mind is more open to the electric uprush of the animal. There is safety in action and unanimity in all the noisy riot of strife – until even that safety is beaten down by the pitiless continuance of physical shock; then there is safety only in the mind again, if it rise like a holy ghost out of the raw stumps of the body.

I remember for a time feeling my heart unrulily beating in my breast, and a tight constriction at the throat. That was perhaps only excitement, or tense expectation of activity. It was not the shuddering grovelling impulse, the sudden jet of pus into the thrilling blood stream, that would sometimes, on the sudden near detonation of a shell, poison one's humanity. That, as I have said, is the only real kind of fear – the purely physical reaction. From that state a few men can recover because they have minds that can surmount a physical state: an imaginative sense of equilibrium. *Imaginative* – it was the men of imagination that were, if any, the men of courage. The men of mere brute strength, the footballers and school captains, found no way out of the inevitable physical reaction. Their bodies broke in fear because the wild energy of the instinct was impinging on a brittle red wall of physical being. That was the feel of it, that was the reality. And P_____? P_____ was in another state of being. Because he had imagination he could visualize and thus anticipate this physical nature of fear. He could immerse himself in the imaginative embodiment of that impulse, and because he had no animal faith he had to succumb to that imaginative condition. Faith was the deepest reality we tested as we crawled for a few minutes along that bank – a few minutes that actually seemed an age. Faith is of many kinds but our faith was simply a level condition of the mind. It might be Christian – sometimes was, I observed. But more often it was just fatalistic, and by fatalism I mean a resolve to live in peace of mind, in possession of mind, despite any physical environment. Such was the faith, or philosophy, that belonged to a great body of men, and was held in very different degrees of intellectuality and passion. In some – they were the majority – it was a reversion to a primitive state of belief. Every bullet has its billet. What's the use of worryin'? But in others it was a subtler state of consciousness. The war seemed to annihilate all sense of individuality. The mass of it was so immense that oneself as a separate unit could not rationally exist. But there is a sense in which the death of individuality means the birth of personality. This truth is the basis of all sacrifice and martyrdom. A saint may die for his faith, but only because that faith is an expression of his personality. And so in the presence of danger, and in the immediate expectation of death, one can forget the body and its fears and exist wholly as a mind.

    We had gone perhaps three parts of our way, when we heard the sound of men working. Muffled coughs, thuds, indefinite clinks. I was nonplussed. The explanation did not immediately occur to me. It hadn't time. I had a sudden sick fear that we must return, empty-handed shameful fools. I think this thought and image lasted the brief interval I had for reflection. For immediately the sergeant tugged my leg and crept close to my ear. He indicated somehow the right. I turned my head. Two figures loomed indistinctly in the dark. Approaching us. 'We must rush them,' I whispered. The sergeant said: 'Right; you give the tip.' The two figures blundered nearer. I could see them hesitate on the other side of the rim of a shell-hole. My heart had suddenly become calm. I was filled with a great exaltation. My body didn't exist, save as a wonderfully unconscious mechanism. I gave a great inhuman cry and dashed forward, barking with my Colt at the shadowy figures not ten yards away. One gave a wild bestial shriek and fell into the darkness. The other fired. We duelled, there in the dark. But I ran on, impelled by an unknown energy, the sergeant by my side. Just then the concerted moment arrived. A dark rainbow of shells hissed through the sky. The flash and detonation of heavy shells. The pale wavering rockets of the star-shells, they curved round us, fell among us. In that incessant theatrical light I saw my enemy dash into the shell-hole at his feet and fall down crying for mercy. I had my foot on the squirming body, sergeant his bayonet. It was an officer. I perceived that quickly, clearly. It was enough. I gave the order: 'Back to the lines.' We turned. The barrage was over now. Only a blind hiss of bullets from the German line. We walked back to the trenches. My men came chattering round, peering with black faces at the prisoner. Prodding him with their bayonets. Crying happily. Lusting to kill him. I tried to keep them off. The prisoner was talking to me, wildly excited. At last he found his French. I understood. He was so pleased! Explained that he was married and had children. He wanted to live. I tried to calm him. He was a professor of philology and lived at Spandau. I took away his revolver; the sergeant took his bright dagger. And thus we reached our own line. As the German hesitated on the parapet someone kicked him violently on the backside, so that he fell down. I cursed the fellow, but didn't stop to identify him. S\_\_\_\_ was there, waiting for me, very much mystified by the turn of events, but jubilant at the sight of a prisoner. We made our way to the headquarters' dugout and descended with our charge.

We blinked in the brilliant light of several candles. It was a square dugout with a fixed table served by benches from the walls. To get to the benches we had to crawl under the table. Our Colonel was a Welshman, temporarily attached from another regiment. When away from the trenches he was pleasant enough, though at bottom a weak and emotional nature. We did not trust him, for he was known to be 'a white-livered funk'. A bottle of whisky was by him on the table, as he sat facing the stairway. He had drunk a great deal, for he was highly nervous about the result of the raid, which would reflect on his reputation. He welcomed us effusively. I don't remember all the chatter and confusion in that confined space, but eventually some kind of order did emerge. D\_\_\_\_\_, our signalling officer, who knew German, began to question the prisoner. The poor fellow was docile enough. He gave up his letters, papers and maps, but asked to keep a photograph of his wife, which we allowed. But a more disgusting scene followed. He had on his finger a signet-ring, perhaps rather a pretty one. The Colonel insisted on having it, and because it would not pass the knuckle, urged us to cut it off. The man was in a delirium and of course we disregarded him. But he made efforts to reach the prisoner himself and in the effort fell drunkenly over and rolled under the table. He lay stupidly there and fell asleep. I watched the prisoner. He was terribly excited, but self-possessed. He was standing against the dark entrance, speaking forcefully and at length. D\_\_\_\_\_ explained to us at intervals. He was passionately defending the German cause, arguing persuasively that we, the English, had been faithless to our common Teutonic stock. The future of Europe was with the German nations; they alone had the energy, the fresh spirit, the nascent culture, for the creation of a new world.

S\_\_\_\_\_ left at about two o'clock to report particulars to the Brigade Headquarters, and at dawn I set out with the prisoner and the happy raiders. We had lost only one man, and there were no serious wounds. We filed-down the communication trenches, leisurely enough, for we were tired. Our faces were still black with the charred cork. The sun rose up to greet us, and when finally we got out into the open country the day was warm and beneficent. The larks were singing again, as on my journey up with P\_\_\_\_\_. But now the sky was pulsing with their shrill notes. On the way I talked to the prisoner and once we rested for a while, sitting side by side on a fallen tree. He explained that when we first surprised them (he was a company officer with his orderly, visiting parties out at work on the battered wire entanglements) they had taken us for Senegalese troops, and his orderly's terror was perhaps largely due to this mistake. But we talked mostly of other things, I was eager to learn anything about their side – their state of mind, their public opinion, the possibility of revolution and an end of all this meaningless strife. Nietzsche was at that time still fresh in my awakening mind, and I stammered in broken enthusiasm about his books, but got no response. He was now too aware of his liberty, his safety, his bodily emancipation to think of such things. He was happy to be safe at last, but perhaps he was also a little chagrined. He was amazed at my youth and perhaps a little ashamed of being captured by what looked like a boyish prank. We strolled again. I only recall his features with difficulty. He was fair and rather short. But I should not know him if I met him again.

    When we reached the Brigade Headquarters I handed him over and stayed to watch him questioned. He stood at attention before a table in the open. And when this was done, he was given into the charge of a guard to be taken down to the Divisional Camp. I last saw him standing at a distance from me, waiting to move. I gazed at him eagerly, tenderly, for I had conceived some sort of vicarious affection for this man. I had done my best to kill him a few hours before. I waved my hand as he left, but he only answered with a vague smile.

    I then made for my battalion reserve and found a hut and a bed. I slept for more than twelve hours and in my sleep, perhaps from weariness, or because of some relaxation in my nerves, my heart seemed to stop and my blood to sweep round in a dark red whirlpool. In my dream I wondered if this was death. But when I awoke I was fresh and content. I was alive. There was light streaming in through the windows, and friendly voices.

# IN RETREAT
## A JOURNAL OF THE RETREAT OF THE FIFTH ARMY FROM ST. QUENTIN, MARCH, 1918*

I

We received the warning order just before dinner, and for a while talked excitedly round the mess fire, some scoffing at the idea of an imminent battle, others gravely saying that this time at any rate the warning was justified. Two deserters, with tales of massing guns and night-movements of innumerable troops, had reached our lines the previous day. Of course deserters usually had some such tale designed to tempt a captor's leniency, but this time it was likely to be the truth. What else could the enemy's long silence mean? To that question we had no answer. We went early to bed, expecting an early awakening. The harnessed horses stood in lowered shafts.

There was scarcely a wall standing in Fluquières: everywhere demolition and bombardment had reduced the village to irregular cairns of brick and plaster. Winding among these cairns were the cleared roadways. Men and horses rested in patched sheds and an occasional cellar. S\_\_\_\_\_ and I were in a small repaired stable, each with a bed-frame in a manger. I had livened the cleanly white-washed walls of the place with illustrations from a coloured magazine. That

---
* See note at end of chapter

evening all save our trench-kit had been sent to the transport-wagons, and we were lying on the bar netting with only our trench coats thrown over us.

For some time I was too excited to sleep, and none too warm. But weariness did at length triumph, and when, a short while afterwards, I was roughly awakened, I had become unconscious enough to forget the continuity of things.

II

Yes: suddenly I was awake. A match was being applied to the candle stuck on the bed-frame above my head. With his excited face illumined in the near candle-light, an orderly bent over me and shook my shoulders. I heard confused shoutings, and the rumble of gunfire. I had hardly need to read the message-form held out to me: 'Man Battle Stations' – the code words I knew only too well, and all that they implied. I was shivering violently with the cold, but in the shaking candle-light I scribbled messages repeating the code to the company commanders, the transport officer and to others. S\_\_\_\_\_ was moving on the other side of the wall that divided the mangers.

    'We're in for it, my lad,' he yelled, above the increasing din. Just then there was a sudden shrieking rush of a descending shell and its riotous detonation very near. Our candles jumped out, and we were in darkness, with bricks and earth falling like a hail on the roof. My servant came in, and hastily helped me to gather my equipment together. He handled the two or three books I always carried with me, asking me if I would take one in my pocket. I took Thoreau's

*Walden,* because I had not yet read it, and anticipated two or three weary days of passive defence. For even if now we realized the actuality of the enemy's attack, so confident were we of our defensive system that we contemplated nothing more than a short successful resistance. When in the front line, we had ceaselessly reconnoitred all approaches, and so fine were the sweeping fields of fire that stretched away towards St Quentin, so skilfully placed were our machine-guns, that always we pitied the folly of the enemy should he assail a defence so deadly. We reckoned with one factor unseen.

I fixed my revolver and ammunition securely, and set out to the orderly room, some five hundred yards away. It was now about five o'clock and still dark. I picked my way along a path which led across the great heaps of rubble. Shells were falling in the village. I still shivered with cold. My electric torch was nearly exhausted, so that I kept falling as I went. When I reached the orderly room, which was in a restored cottage, I found everything in a great hubbub, orderlies coming and going, the sergeant-major shouting orders. Inside, the doctor was bandaging a wounded man.

S____, who had been assembling the headquarter staff, came to say that something terrible had happed to the Lewis team (at that time a Lewis-gun team was attached to each battalion headquarters): would I come round with my torch.

They had been sleeping, some six men, beneath tarpaulin sheets, stretched across a half-demolished out-house. A shell had fallen in the middle of them. In the weak glare of my torch, we saw a mangled mass of red brick-dust and of red glistening blood. Here and there we distinguished a tousled head of hair. One man, pinned beneath beams and brickwork, was still groaning. We quickly began to extricate him, but he died whilst we worked.

I then joined the colonel, and with one or two orderlies and the sergeant-major we followed the companies along the back lane that led from Fluquières to Roupy, a distance of about a mile and a half. The morning was cold and a heavy dew lay on the ground. As we walked the light of dawn began to reveal a thick wet mist.

III

At 6.50 I sent a message to the brigade, informing them that the battalion was in position. We had been shelled all along the way, and when we neared Roupy, the cross-roads seemed to be under a continuous barrage. Nevertheless, we got into position with very few casualties. Safe in the bowels of the headquarter dugout, we thought the worst was over, and began casually to eat the tongue sandwiches and drink the tea provided by the mess-corporal.

The dugout was new and spacious, and odorous of the fresh chalky earth. It was about thirty feet deep, and partitioned into three sections, of which the middle one was occupied by the headquarter officers. Because it was new it was unfurnished, and we had to squat on the bare floor, grouped round a few candles.

For me that cavern is a telephonic nightmare. The instrument, a 'D III converted', was placed on the floor in a corner of the dugout. Two signallers sat with their legs straddling round it. At first the companies, then the neighbouring battalions, and, finally, the brigade, kept me there crouching on the floor, yelling till I was hoarse into the execrable instrument. When I was not speaking, the signallers were receiving or sending Morse messages.

Above the ground the situation was disquieting. The thick mist of the early dawn persisted: a man ten yards away could not be distinguished. The gunfire, tremendous in its intensity, continued hour after hour to pound into the invisible foreground. The earth vibrated almost hysterically. An occasional shell crashed near us, but after the first three hours (at 7.30) the enemy's fire seemed to be concentrated on our front-line defences. No messages, telephonic or written, came to relieve our anxiety.

The gradual accumulation of our anxiety should be realized. Every minute seemed to add to its intensity. By ten o'clock or so, our hearts were like taut drum skins beaten reverberantly by every little incident.

Then the skin smashed. Bodily action flickered the flame, the sense of duration was consumed away.

Shortly after eleven o'clock, a gun team galloped madly down the main road. Then two stragglers belonging to the Machine-Gun Corps were brought to headquarters. They informed us that the front line had been penetrated. Later, an officer from the front line battalion, with five or six men, came to us out of the mist. Most of the party were wounded, and as the officer's leg was being bandaged in the dugout, he told us his tale. He was haggard and incoherent, but the sequence was awfully clear to us. The enemy had attacked in great strength at 7.30. They had apparently reached the observation line unobserved, and overpowered the few men there before a warning could be given or an escape made. Advancing under cover of a creeping barrage, they had approached the main line of defence. No fire met them there, or only fire directed vaguely into the fog. The fight at the main line had been short and bloody. Our men, dazed and quivering after three hours' hellish bombardment (I could see them cowering on the cold mist-wet earth), had been brave to the limits of heroism; but pitifully powerless. The ghastly job had been completed by 8.30. About nine o'clock fresh enemy battalions passed through their fellows and advanced towards the front-line redoubt (L'Épine de Dallon). Our artillery fire must have been useless by then, still falling on the old enemy front line. At any rate, the enemy quickly surrounded the redoubt, and then penetrated it. This officer himself had been captured, and later had made his escape in the mist. He thought it possible that the headquarters of his battalion were still holding out.

We were still questioning our informant when an excited voice yelled down the dugout shaft: 'Boches on the top of the dugout.' Our hearts thumped. There was no reason why the enemy shouldn't be on us. They might have been anywhere in that damned mist. We drew revolvers and rushed to the shaft. We did not mean to be caught like rats in a hole.

I remember my emotion distinctly: a quiet despair. I *knew* I went up those stairs either to be shot or bayoneted as I emerged, or, perhaps, to be made prisoner and so plunge into a strange unknown existence.

Half-way up the stairs, and a voice cried down: 'It's all right: they're our fellows.' Some artillerymen in overcoats, straggling across the open, had looked sinister in the mist.

We turned to the dugout, the released tension leaving us exhausted.

Patrols from our front companies had been feeling outward all morning, at first without result. At 12.30 B\_\_\_\_\_

(commanding the left front company) reported: 'Machine-gun and rifle-fire on left and right can be heard. Shelling very hard. Can see nothing. Patrols are being sent out.' At 1 pm he reported: 'Boche are in quarry just in front of me. We are firing Lewis guns and rifles at him. He seems to be firing from our right flank too, with machine-guns.'

These and other messages all came by runner. The telephonic communications to the companies had broken down before noon, though I think we remained in touch with the brigade until late in the afternoon.

About midday the mist began to clear a little. At one o'clock the enemy, having massed in the valley five hundred yards immediately in front of us, attacked in mass strength. The fusillade that met them must have been terrific. They came on in good order, extending and manoeuvring with precision. At 1.20 B_____ reported: 'No. 5 Platoon report enemy on wire in front. Artillery assistance is asked for. We are firing rifle grenades into them.' And again at 1.30: 'Boche attacking in strength with sections in front. Front troops are in valley in front. They are also heading to my left flank'. Between 1.30 and 1.40 the attack reached its greatest intensity. By 1.45 it had withered completely before the hail of our fire.

At 1.45 B_____ reported: 'Boche running back like hell near Savy. They seem to be running from artillery as much as anything.' (Savy was one and a half miles to our left front: it was on the slope that rose away from the valley in front of us where the enemy had massed his forces before his attack.)

For a moment we became elated. There was cause enough. The mist had lifted, and a pale sun shone. We had defeated a strong attack. We received a message from the

Inniskillings on our right to say they still held their positions intact. And wider afield the co-ordination of the enemy's advance seemed to have broken down.

We have made hast to distribute our reserve ammunition, to clear the dressing-station, and generally to make ourselves ready for the next happenings.

In reply to my inquiries B_____ sent this message, timed 2.15 pm: 'It is very difficult to tell numbers of enemy. I can see the ground north to Savy, and saw them scattered. The line advancing had about 30 men to every 100 yards. We do not require SAA yet. Can you instruct Rose *[code name for a company]* to fire up Soup Valley, please? We will want Very lights for the night. Will a supply be forthcoming? Can see no movement now. Boche is putting up white lights all along valley.'

IV

The lull was not of long duration. Either we had been deceived by the movements near Savy, or the enemy had made a miraculously swift recovery. At 2.45 I received another message from B_____: 'Enemy movement at F. 12 at 4.0. They appear to be carrying in wounded. Enemy also advancing across valley on left on F. 5, in small parties. Estimated total strength seen, 50 men. Boche aeroplanes are flying about 300 feet above our lines, and have been for a short while past. There is still some machine-gun fire in front. Is a redoubt holding out?'

The aeroplanes were evidently making a preliminary reconnaissance, and I guessed the movement to be significant of a new attack.

On the mists clearing, the aeroplanes were able to sight position, and soon the artillery on both sides became active. Our own artillery, alas, fired short, smashing our already weakened defences. The Germans brought up their light field guns with great skill and rapidity. Several batteries were observed coming over the ridge at L'Épine de Dallon - only a few hours ago the headquarters of the battalion we were supporting. We now realized our position in earnest, and I sent a detailed account of the situation to the brigade.

Towards four o'clock, the enemy shelling increased in intensity. The second attack was now imminent. B_____ sent the following message, timed 4.30 pm. 'Boche is attacking on right about 400 strong, and is massing in the valley right in front of Roupy. We want some more SAA. During the Boche retreat the riflemen and Lewis guns did good work, killing many. Shelling very heavy.'

The heavy shelling continued, and under cover of its intensity the enemy again massed in the valley in front of us. The men held on grimly. Thus B____, timed 5.10 pm: 'Line holding still with some casualties. Reports not in. Line heavily shelled. SAA received correct. Situation still the same. Touch is being kept with battalion on our right, and patrols go constantly. Our chloride of lime is missing and cannot be found. Machine-guns very active.' And again at 5.40 pm: 'The Boche is 50 yards or less from our line, and is also passing down the valley for another attack.'

Then suddenly those massed men leapt from cover, and came on in their grey, regular formations. At headquarters we were only aware of the angry surge of rifle and machine-gun fire, deadening even the detonations of shells. All this time I was spending tiring, exasperating hours at the telephone, striving to get in communication with brigade and artillery headquarters. Again and again the wire was broken, and again and again the linesmen went out into the mist to mend it. Then it got disconnected irreparably. We were isolate in that chaos.

About 6.30 B\_\_\_\_\_ sent the following momentous message: 'Boche got inside our wire on right and left. No. 5 Platoon are all either wiped out or prisoners. No. 7 Platoon took up position on left of keep, but Boche were in it when I left. They also were in trench on right of road left by C. Company, and we killed several on road near camouflage. I am now in redoubt with 25 men.'

The climax had come. We had still one card to play – the counter-attack company. On receipt of B\_\_\_\_\_'s message, the colonel decided to order C\_\_\_\_\_ to attack in accordance with the pre-conceived plan.

We only heard of this counter-attack from the mouths of a few survivors. It was one of the most heroic episodes in the retreat. The company gathered together in the shell-battered trench that they had occupied all day, and then took the open. No artillery covered their advance. It was hopeless, insane, suicidal. They had perhaps one hundred and fifty yards to cover. They advanced at a jog-trot, lumbering on the uneven ground. One by one they fell before the fusillade that met them. C\_\_\_\_\_ had reached the enemy with about a dozen men. These leapt in among the Boches, and a hand-to-hand struggle ensued for a few minutes. C\_\_\_\_\_ was last seen cursing, pinned to the trench wall by a little mob of Germans, in one hand his empty smoking revolver.

## V

It was now dusk, and with dusk came peace and silence. And at dusk this was our position – The front rim of the redoubt was in the enemy's possession. The counter-attack company had disappeared. The company-keeps still held out with a few men in each. The inner ring of the redoubt was held by one company, and the remnants of three. B_____ had survived with one of his officers. But several officers in the three front companies had been either killed, wounded or captured. There were probably two hundred men still surviving in the battalion.

In the darkness the colonel and I walked up to the line. As we went along the road, the stillness was abruptly broken by the sound of three or four shots, screams and curses. We flung ourselves on the roadside, our revolvers ready. We shouted: 'Who goes there?' English voices answered, and the sergeant-major went to investigate. Two German privates had walked into a sentry on the road, *coming from behind us*. No one could understand what they said, and they were sent back to brigade headquarters. And I don't remember that any one of us was perturbed by the incident, eerie though it was.

Just after one o'clock in the morning, we received long-awaited instructions from the brigade. The battalion in reserve was to deliver a counter-attack. The line of deployment was given, and the direction of attack. The battalion was to leave its position at 12.45, and the guns were to start a creeping barrage at 1.33 am.

The whole thing was a ghastly failure. The night was black, and the battalion attacking was unfamiliar with the ground it had to cover. We waited hours for a sign of their approach. About two o'clock a stray officer came to us, having lost his company. Eventually, about four o'clock, one company did appear. It went forward in the darkness, but got dispersed and uncontrollable in the effort to deploy into attack formation. Dawn found us as dusk had found us, with the sole difference that some two hundred men of the counter-attack battalion had found refuge in our redoubt, and in the keeps in front.

I think by then we were past hope or despair. We regarded all events with an indifference of weariness, knowing that with the dawn would come another attack. We distributed ammunition, reorganized our Lewis guns, and waited dully, without apprehension.

Again the morning was thickly misty. Our own artillery fire was desultory and useless. Under cover of the mist, the enemy massed in battle formation, and the third attack began about 7 am. We only heard a babel in the mist. Now our artillery was firing short among our men in the redoubt. About ten o'clock the enemy penetrated our left flank, presumably in the gap between us and the battalion on our left, which was still in position. Machine-gun fire began to harass us from that direction, somewhere in the ruins of the village. We never heard from the battalion on our right, and a runner I sent there did not return. I think they must have withdrawn about ten o'clock.

This new attack petered out. I fancy it was only half-hearted on the part of the enemy – probably only a demonstration to see if we intended to make a determined resistance, or to fight only a rearguard action. Finding the resistance determined enough, they evidently retired to prepare the real thing.

This fourth attack was delivered about midday. The mist still persisted thinly. One could perhaps see objects fifty yards away. I don't know what resistance the platoon-keeps offered. They were in a hopeless position, and would easily have been swamped in a massed attack.

Shortly after midday, the enemy came in direct contact with the inner ring of the redoubt.

We fired like maniacs. Every round of ammunition had been distributed. The Lewis guns jammed; rifle bolts grew stiff and unworkable with the expansion of heat.

In the lull before noon, the colonel and I had left the dugout, in which we were beginning to feel like rats in a trap, and had found an old gun-pit about two hundred and fifty yards farther back, and here we established our headquarters. An extraordinary thing happened. The gun-pit was dug out of the bank on the roadside. About two o'clock one of our guns, evidently assuming that Roupy had been evacuated, began to pound the road between Roupy and Fluquères. One of these shells landed clean on the road edge of our pit. We were all hurled to the ground by the explosion, but, on recovering ourselves, found only one casualty: the colonel had received a nasty gash in the forearm. We then went two hundred to three hundred yards across the open, away from the road, and found a smaller over-grown pit. The colonel refused to regard his wound as serious; but he soon began to feel dizzy, and was compelled to go back to the dressing-station. I was then left in charge of the battalion.

It was now about 2.30. The attack still persisted in a guerrilla fashion. But the enemy was massing troops in the trenches already taken. At 4 pm the intensity of the attack deepened suddenly. A new intention had come into the enemy's mind: he was directing his attack on the flanks of our position in an effort to close round us like pincers. On the left he made use of cover offered by the ruined village, and eventually brought machine-guns to bear against us from our left rear. On the right he made use of the trenches evacuated by the Inniskillings.

In the height of this attack, while my heart was heavy with anxiety, I received a message from the brigade. Surely reinforcements were coming to our aid! Or was I at length given permission to withdraw? Neither: it was a rhetorical appeal to hold on to the last man. I rather bitterly resolved to obey the command.

Another hour passed. The enemy pressed on relentlessly with a determined, insidious energy, reckless of cost. Our position was now appallingly precarious. I therefore resolved to act independently, and do as perhaps I should have done hours earlier. I ordered B_____ to organize a withdrawal. This message dispatched I lay on my belly in the grass and watched through my field glasses every minute trickling of the enemy's progress. Gradually they made their way round the rim of the redoubt, bombing along the traverses. And now we only held it as lips might touch the rim of a saucer. I could see the heads of my men, very dense and in a little space. And on either side, incredibly active, gathered the grey helmets of the Germans. It was like a long bowstring along the horizon, and our diminished forces the arrow to be shot into a void. A great many hostile machine-guns had now been brought up, and the plain was sprayed with hissing bullets. They impinged and spluttered about the little pit in which I crouched.

I waited anxiously for B_____ to take the open. I saw men crawl out of the trenches, and lie flat on the parados, still firing at the enemy. Then, after a little while, the arrow was launched. I saw a piteous band of men rise from the ground, and run rapidly towards me. A great shout went up from the Germans: a cry of mingled triumph and horror. 'Halt Eenglisch!' they cried, and for a moment were too amazed to fire; as though aghast at the folly of men who could plunge into such a storm of death. But the first silent gasp of horror expended, then broke the crackling storm. I don't remember in the whole war an intenser taste of hell. My men came along spreading rapidly to a line of some two hundred yards length, but bunched here and there. On the left, by the main road, the enemy rushed out to cut them off. Bayonets clashed there. Along the line men were falling swiftly as the bullets hit them. Each second they fell, now one crumpling up, now two or three at once. I saw men stop to pick up their wounded mates, and as they carried them along, themselves get hit and fall with their inert burdens. Now they were near me, so I rushed out of my pit and ran with them to the line of trenches some three hundred yards behind.

    It seemed to take a long time to race across those few hundred yards. My heart beat nervously, and I felt infinitely weary. The bullets hissed about me, and I thought: then this is the moment of death. But I had no emotions. I remembered having read how in battle men are hit, and never feel the hurt till later, and I wondered if I had yet been hit. Then I reached the line. I stood petrified, enormously aghast. *The trench had not been dug, and no reinforcements occupied it.* It was as we had passed it on the morning of the 21st, the sods dug off the surface, leaving an immaculately patterned 'mock' trench. A hundred yards on the right a machine-gun corps had taken up a position, and was already covering our retreat. I looked about me wildly, running along the line and signalling to the men to drop as they reached the slender parapet of sods. But the whole basis of my previous tactics had been destroyed. I should never have ordered my men to cross that plain of death, but for the expectation that we were falling back to reinforce a new line. We found an empty mockery, and I was in despair. But I must steady the line. On the actual plain the men obeyed my signals, and crouched in the shallow trench. But even as they crouched, the bullets struck them. On the road, the straight white road leading to the western safety, there was something like a stampede. S_____ and the sergeant-major went and held it with pointed revolvers. But it was all useless – hopeless. On the right, I saw the enemy creeping round. They would soon enfilade us, and then our shallow defence would be a death-trap. I accordingly gave the signal to withdraw, bidding the two Lewis guns to cover us as long as possible. Once more we rose and scattered in retreat. It would be about seven hundred yards to the next trenches – the village line round Fluquères – and this we covered fairly well, sections occasionally halting to give covering fire. The enemy had not yet ventured from the redoubt, and our distance apart was now great enough to make his fire of little effect. And I think as we moved up the slope towards the village we must have been in 'dead' ground, so far as the enemy advancing on the right was concerned.

    We reached Fluquères, which lay on the top of the slope, and found there some deep trenches on each side of the road at the entrance of the village. Further to the left, I found certain London troops commanded by a major. One of my Lewis guns still remained intact, and this I placed to fire down the straight road to Roupy. The enemy had now left the redoubt and were advancing in line formation.

We were at Fluquères about an hour. The enemy evidently did not intend to rest content with his capture of the redoubt. It was just beginning to get dusk. Earlier we had noticed sporadic contact lights go up. But now they shot into the sky from all along the plain. Low-flying aeroplanes hovered over the advancing line, and their wireless messages soon put the German guns on to us. Big black high-explosive shells began to fall on our position, making our tired flesh shudder. I now began to be amazed at the advancing contact lights. They did not merely stretch in a line in front of us: *they encircled us like a horse-shoe, the points of which seemed* (and actually were) *miles behind us*. On the right the enemy was enfilading us with machine-gun fire.

I searched for the major commanding the troops on my left, but could not find him. By this time I was determined to act, and therefore gave the order to withdraw. The men filed through the village, gathering fresh ammunition from a dump at the crossroads. From the village the road went up a slope leading to Aubigny. The enemy's fire soon followed us, and we proceeded along the ditches on each side of the road.

Three-quarters of the way up the slope I observed a trench running at right-angles to the road on each side of it. I ordered the London men to go to the left, my own to the right, there to reorganize into companies. The twilight was now fairly deep, and I thought that with evening the enemy's advance would stay. The major I had seen in Fluquères now appeared again, and cursed me for giving the order to retire. I was too tired to argue, and even then a gust of machine-gun fire swept above our heads. They were going to attack again.

We could hear them moving in the semi-darkness. Something else we could hear too – the throb of a motorcycle behind us. It was a dispatch rider, and when he drew level to us, he stopped his machine and came towards me with a message. I opened it. It ordered all troops east of the Aubigny defences to retire through Ham.

I was glad. I believe I thought then that it was the end of our share in the battle. I went to the men, and assembled them in companies, and in close artillery formation we retired across country due west. We came to the Aubigny defences, manned by fresh troops, about a mile further on, and then we gathered on the road again and marched wearily along. I remember coming to a water-tank, where we all drank our fill – our mouths were swollen with thirst. When we reached Ham, an officer met us and ordered us to proceed to Muille Villette, about two miles further on, and there billet for the night. Ham, as we walked through its cobbled streets seemed very hollow and deserted. The last time we had seen it, it had been a busy market-town, full of civilians. Now only a few sinister looters went about the empty houses with candles. We saw one fellow come out of a door with a lady's reticule and other things over his arm. We should have been justified in shooting him, but we were far too tired. We just noticed him stupidly.

The road seemed long, and our pace was slow, but at last we reached the village of Muille Villette. We found it fully of artillerymen, and a few infantry. Every available shelter seemed to be occupied, but at length we got the men into a school. Our transport had been warned of our station for the night, and turned up with bully-beef and biscuits. These we served out.

I had four officers left with me. We could not find a billet for ourselves, but finally begged for shelter in a barn occupied by artillerymen. They looked on us unsympathetically, not knowing our experiences. On a stove one of them was cooking a stew of potatoes and meat, and its savour made us lusting beasts. But the artillery men ate the slop unconcernedly, while we lay down too utterly weary to sleep, languidly chewing bully-beef.

VI

It was after midnight when we came to Muille Villette; I suppose about 2 am we fell into an uneasy sleep. At 4 am we were awakened by the stirrings and shoutings of the artillerymen. I drew my long boots on my aching feet, and went out into the cold darkness. I found an officer of some kind. The enemy were reported to have attacked and penetrated the Aubigny defences, and to be now advancing on Ham. All the troops stationed in Muille Villette had received orders to withdraw.

We assembled the men, stupid with sleep. I knew that brigade headquarters were stationed at Golancourt, a mile and a half along the road. I resolved to proceed there and ask for orders. We marched away while the dawn was breaking.

I found the brigade established in a deserted house. T\_\_\_\_\_, the brigade-major, was seated on a bed lacing his boots. No orders for the brigade had yet been received, so T\_\_\_\_\_ advised me to find billets for the men, where they could rest and get food. The companies then sought billets independently, and, what was more blessed than anything, we managed to get them hot tea. I went and had breakfast with the brigade staff. The tea revived me, and I remember how voracious I felt, and that I tried to hide this fact. The brigadier came into the room and seemed very pleased to see me: apparently he was very satisfied with our conduct, and especially with the frequent reports I had sent back. Till then I had only felt weariness and bafflement – even shame. But now I began to see that we were implicated in something immense – something beyond personal feelings and efforts.

    The brigadier told me as much as he knew of the general situation. It was not much. The communications had apparently broken down. But it was enough to make me realize that more than a local attack was in progress: the whole of the Fifth Army was involved: but there were no limits to what *might* be happening.

    I also learnt that Drury – where the divisional headquarters had been stationed – a village some five or six miles south-*west* of Roupy, had been captured about two o'clock on the afternoon of the 22nd, several hours before we had evacuated the redoubt. Only a miracle of chance had saved us from being cut off.

    The brigade seemed to have difficulty in getting into touch with the division, or, at any rate, in obtaining orders from them. But at 10 am I was told to march to Freniches and await orders there. We assembled in the village street and marched on again. The road was busy with retreating artillery and a few infantrymen. From behind us came the sounds of firing: the enemy were attacking Ham. We trudged on, passing villages whose inhabitants were only just taking steps to flee. They piled beds, chairs, and innumberable bolsters on little carts, some hand-pulled, some yoked to bony horses. They tied cows behind. There were old men, many old women, a few young women, but no young men. They and their like proceeded with us along the western road.

We had gone perhaps five miles when an orderly on horseback overtook us with orders. We were to report to the —th Division at Freniches.

This we eventually did, and a fat staff colonel studied a map, and then told me to take my battalion to Esmery-Hallon, a village four miles due north, and there take up a defensive position. This was more than I expected. I explained that my men had been fighting continuously for forty-eight hours, and were beaten and spiritless. But I received no comfort: the situation demanded that every available man should be used to the bitter end. I hardly dared to face my men: but I think they were too tired to mind where they went. We turned off at a right-angle, and slowly marched on. The road led through a beautiful patch of country, steeped in a calm, liquid sunshine. We tilted our bodies forward, and forced our weary muscles to act.

About two miles south of Esmery-Hallon, an officer (a lieutenant) appeared on a motor cycle. He was in command of a scrap lot – transport men, cobblers, returned leave men, etc. He seemed to have the impression that the enemy were upon us, and wanted me to deploy and take up a position facing east. I explained that we were much too tired to do any such thing. He expostulated. Did I realize this, that, and the other? I explained that I had cause to realize such things better than he did. He raved. I told him finally that I didn't care a damn, but that I had orders to defend Esmery-Hallon, and thither I must go. He went off in a rage, seeming incredibly silly and fussy to us all.

Esmery-Hallon is a small village perched on a detached conical hill, overlooking the plain on all sides. The defence was simply arranged. Two companies of engineers were entrenched in front of the village. I sent a look-out on to the top of the church tower, and extended my men astraddle the hill on each side of the village, north and south. The men on the south found a ditch, which made an admirable trench. The men on the north extended over the ploughed land, and dug shallow pits for shelter. We had no machine-guns or Lewis guns, but every man had a rifle and a decent amount of ammunition. I established my headquarters on the north side by a quarry, where I had a wide view of the plain.

The day was very still, and the distant rattle of machine-gun fire carried to us. A few enemy shells fell ineffectively about the landscape. I got into touch with a major of the Inniskillings in command of one hundred and fifty men on my right, and we co-ordinated defences on that wing. My left wing was in the air, so to speak – not a soul visible for miles.

When our dispositions were finally made, I returned to the quarry edge. My servant T_____ had already been away to search the village and now came laden with samples of red wine and cider which he had found in a cellar. So I sent him back to the village with other men, telling them to search for food also. They soon returned with bottles of red wine and a large tin of army biscuits. Evidently there was any amount of wine, but I was afraid to distribute it among the men for fear lest on fasting stomachs it should make them drunk. So S_____ and I each took a wine glass, and starting at different points, we begun to go a round of the men. Each man lay curled up in his shallow pit, resting. To each we gave a glass of wine and a few biscuits. They took it thankfully. There was a lull in the distant fighting: I don't remember any noise of fire during that hour. The sun was warm and seemed to cast a golden peace on the scene. A feeling of unity with the men about me suddenly suffused my mind.

VII

It was nearly two o'clock when we got settled. About this time I interrupted a message which gave me the useful information that the enemy had been seen in Ham at 10 am. I guessed that the silence meant they were now consolidating along the Somme Canal. Later in the afternoon a cavalry patrol trotted up to our position. Officer, men, and horses all looked very debonair and well fed. The officer was very condescending towards me, but made a message of the information I gave him, thought it would not be worth while venturing further on to the plain, so rode away back, harness jingling, the sun shining on well-polished accoutrements.

About five o'clock, I judged that we were to be left alone for the night, and made my plans accordingly. I sent the following message to B_____, who was in charge of the men on the right of the village: 'We hold on to our present positions unless otherwise ordered. When it is getting dark close your men in a little to form about 7 or 8 pickets. From these pickets send standing patrols out about 150 yards, or to any good observation point within warning distance. Any show of resistance should drive off any enemy patrols. But as far as I can make out the Boche is still east of the canal. Should you be attacked by overwhelming numbers, withdraw fighting in a due westerly direction under your own arrangements. I should do the same in case of need. I suggest you come up to have a look at our position before dark.'

But just after dark, I received orders to relieve the Royal Engineers in front of the village. I regretted this order, but had to obey it. We now found ourselves in freshly dug trenches on the flat of the plain, our view to the left and right obstructed by woods.

Included in the orders mentioned was a message to the effect that advance parties of the French would probably arrive that night, and the positions would be shown to them. This message filled us with wild hope; we became almost jaunty.

But the night was very cold, and heavily wet with dew. We improved the trenches, and stamped about, flapping our arms in an effort to keep warm. I sat with L\_\_\_\_\_ , bravest and brightest of my runners, on a waterproof sheet beneath a tree in the centre of our position. We waited for the dawn: it was weird, phantasmagorical. Again the fateful mist. As it cleared a little, the woods near us hung faintly in the whiteness.

At 8am we began to observe troops retreating in front of us. They came in little groups down the road, or straggled singly over the landscape. The mist gradually lifted. We heard machine-gun fire fairly near, somewhere on the right. The stragglers informed us that the enemy had crossed the canal in the early dawn, and was advancing in considerable force. We waited patiently. At 9 am the enemy came into touch with our fellows on the left, and here we rebutted him successfully. At 9.30 the troops on our right were reported to be withdrawing. About ten o'clock, there happened one of those sudden episodes, which would be almost comic with their ludicrous *bouleversement* were they not so tragic in their results. Seemingly straight from the misty sky itself, but in reality from our own guns, descended round after round of shrapnel bursting terrifically just above our heads, and spraying leaden showers upon us. Simultaneously, from the woods on our right, there burst a fierce volley of machine-gun fire, hissing and spluttering among us. We just turned and fled into the shelter of the village buildings. I shouted to my men to make for the position of the quarry. We scuttled through gardens and over walls. By the time we reached the quarry we had recovered our nerve. We extended and faced the enemy, who were advancing skilfully over the plain on our left. We on our part were a scrap lot composed of various units. We hastily reorganized into sections. Retreat was inevitable. Then followed a magnificent effort of discipline. A major took charge of the situation, and we began to retire with covering fire, section by section, in perfect alternation.

We were now on a wide expanse of plain, sloping gently westward. We stretched over this – a thin line of men, perhaps a thousand yards long. We were approaching the Nesle-Noyon Canal. When within a few hundred yards of the canal, we closed inwards to cross a bridge (Ramecourt). At the other end of the bridge stood a staff officer, separating the men like sheep as they crossed, first a few to the left, then a few to the right. Here I got separated from the majority of my men, finding myself with only fifteen. We were told to proceed along the bank of the canal until we found an unoccupied space, and there dig in.

As we crossed the bridge, we saw for the first time the sky-blue helmets of the French troops peeping above a parapet. I think our eyes glistened with expectation of relief.

We went perhaps half a mile along the bank of the canal, and there I halted my attenuated company. The sun was now blazing hotly above our heads. We dropped to the ground, utterly exhausted. Presently some of the men began spontaneously to dig. R\_\_\_\_\_, the only officer left with me, also took a pick and joined the men. I began to feel ashamed just then, for I would willingly have died. I took a spade (there was a dump of such things just by us) and began to shovel the earth loosened by R\_\_\_\_\_. I seemed to be lifting utterly impossible burdens. My flesh seemed to move uneasily through iron bands; my leaden lids drooped smartingly upon my eyes.

We dug about three feet, and then ceased, incapable of more. At the foot of the bank there was a small pool of water. The enemy was not now in sight, so we plunged our hot faces and hands into its weedy freshness, and took off our boots and socks, and bathed our aching feet.

In the evening, about 5 pm, a few skirmishing patrols appeared on the horizon. But our artillery was now active and fairly accurate, and machine-guns swept the plain. The patrols retired, without having advanced any distance. A large German aeroplane, with a red belly, floated persistently above our line. We fired hundreds of shots at it, but without effect. T\_\_\_\_\_, my batman, nearly blew my head off in his efforts.

We had gathered a lot of sun-scorched hemlock and bedded the bottom of our trenches; and when night came on we posted sentries, and huddled down to the bedding. The night was clear, and I gazed unblinkingly at the fierce stars above me, my aching flesh forbidding sleep. Later, I must have dozed in a wakeful stupor.

## VIII

The next daybreak, that of the 25th, was less misty. Bread and bully-beef had come up during the night, and we fed to get warmth into our bodies. But the sun was soon up, and we began to feel almost cheerful once again. There was no immediate sign of the enemy, and I walked along to the bridge we had crossed the previous day to glean some information of our intentions; but the only plan seemed to be the obvious one of holding on to our positions. I noticed some engineers were there ready to blow up the bridge if need be.

About 8am we saw little groups of enemy cavalry appear on the horizon. Through my glasses I could see them consulting maps, pointing, trotting fussily about. Our artillery was planting some kind of scattered barrage on the plain, and an occasional nearshot made the horsemen scamper. We watched them rather amusedly till ten o'clock and then we saw signs of infantrymen. They came from the direction of Esmery-Hallon, and at first seemed in fairly dense formation. But they extended as they cut the sky line, and we soon perceived them advancing in open order. As they got nearer, they began to organize short rushes, a section at a time.

We were now well stocked with ammunition – there were piles of it lying about – and as soon as the advancing troops were within anything like range, we began to 'pot' them. In fact, the whole thing became like a rifle-gallery entertainment at a fair. But still they came on. Now we could see them quite plainly – could see their legs working like dancing bears, and their great square packs bobbing up and down as they ran. Occasionally one dropped.

Immediately in front of our trench, about eight hundred yards away, there was a little copse of perhaps fifty trees. This they reached about eleven o'clock and halted there. If only our flanks held out, I guessed they would never get farther, for between the copse and our rifles and Lewis guns there was not a shred of cover; and we were well entrenched, with a wide canal in front of us.

Of course, the artillery was busy all the while: not methodically, but thickly enough to give the day the appearance of a conventional battle. But then the unexpected (really we had no cause longer to regard it as unexpected), the fatal thing happened. A battery of ours shortened its range, and got our position exactly 'taped'. The shells fell thick and fast, right into our backs. We were, remember, dug in on the top of a bank, perhaps fifteen feet high. All along this bank the shells plunged. Immediately on our right, not fifty yards away, a shell landed cleanly into a trench, and when the smoke cleared there remained nothing, absolutely nothing distinguishable, where a moment ago had been five or six men. We grovelled like frightened, cowed animals. Still the shells fell: and there was no means of stopping them. I glanced distractedly round; men on the right were running under cover of the bank away to the right. Other men on the left were retreating to the left. I resolved to get out of it. Immediately behind us, fifty yards away, was a large crescent-shaped mound, very steep, like a railway embankment, and perhaps sixty feet high. It occurred to me that from there we should command, and command as effectively as ever, the plain in front of us. I made my intention known, and at a given signal we leapt down the bank, and across the intervening fifty yards. We were evidently in sight, for a hail of machine-gun bullets made dusty splutters all round us as we ran. But we reached the mound without a casualty, and climbed safely on to it. There I found a few men already in occupation, commanded by a colonel, under whose orders I then placed myself.

The enemy's artillery fire now increased in volume. I saw a cow hit in a field behind us, and fall funnily with four rigid legs poking up at the sky.

At 3.30 we saw the French retiring on the right, about a thousand yards away. They were not running, but did not seem to be performing any methodic withdrawal. We then fell into one of those awful states of doubt and indecision. What was happening? What should we do? There was angry, ominous rifle-fire on our immediate left. About 4 pm there was a burst of machine-gun fire on our immediate right. I noticed that the stray bullets were coming over our heads. This meant that the enemy were advancing from the right.

I then saw English troops withdrawing about six hundred yards away on the right – evidently the troops that had been defending the bridge. I did not hear any explosion, and so far as I know the bridge remained intact.

At 4.15 I saw the colonel with his men suddenly leave his position on my immediate left. Although I was within sight – within calling distance – he did not give me an order. I was now alone on the mound with my fifteen men.

I did not wait long. I resolved to act on my own initiative once more. We had now moved off the maps I possessed and might as well be in an unknown wilderness. I resolved to proceed due west, taking the sun as a guide. We moved down the back slope of the mound. At the foot we found a stream or off-flow from the canal, about ten feet wide and apparently very deep. As we hesitated, looking for a convenient crossing, a machine-gun a few hundred yards away opened fire on us. There were a good few trees about which must have obstructed the firer's view: the cut twigs, newly budded, fell into the water. We hesitated no longer: we plunged into the stream. The men had to toss their rifles across, many of which landed short and were lost. The sight of these frightened men plunging into the water effected one of those curious stirrings of the memory that call up some vivid scene of childhood: I saw distinctly the water-rats plunging at dusk into the mill-dam at Thornton-le-Dale, where I had lived as a boy of ten.

    The water sucked at my clothes as I met it, and filled my field boots. They seemed weighted with lead now as I walked, and oozed for hours afterwards.

    We came out facing a wide plain, climbing gently westward. Machine-gun and rifle-fire still played about us. We could see a church steeple on the horizon due west, and I told the men to scatter and make for that steeple. Shrapnel was bursting in the sky, too high to be effective. We ran a little way, but soon got too tired. A\_\_\_\_\_, a faithful orderly, had stayed with me, and soon we walked over the fields as friends might walk in England. We came across French machine-gunners, who looked at us curiously, asked for news of the situation, but did not seem very perturbed.

    We eventually came to the village on the horizon (probably Solente). An officer of the engineers stood by the side of his horse at the cross-roads, smoking a cigarette. He asked me why I was retreating. The question seemed silly: 'We shall have to fight every inch of the way back again,' he said. 'These Frenchmen will never hold them.' I went on, too tired to answer.

Here I saw for the first time a new post stuck on the roadside. It had on it an arrow and 'Stragglers Post' in bold letters. So I was a straggler. I felt very bitter and full of despair.

I followed the road indicated by the arrow. It was dotted with small parties of men, all dejected and weary. We trudged along till we came to the village of Carrepuits. Military police met us at the entrance, and told us to report to the Traffic Control in a house a few hundred yards away. It was now getting dusk. I went into the cottage indicated, and here found an officer, very harassed and bored. Men were collected, and separated into the divisions they belonged to, and then given orders to report to such and such a place. I found a party of about fifty men of my division, and was instructed to take them and report to a divisional headquarters situated in a certain street in Roye.

I've forgotten that walk: it was only about two miles, but our utter dejection induced a kind of unconsciousness in us. It would be between ten and eleven o'clock when we got to Roye. I reported to the staff officer, who sent me off to the town major to get billets. The town major I found distracted, unable to say where I should find a billet. Apparently the town was packed with stragglers. We peered into two great gloomy marquees, floored densely with recumbent men. Meanwhile two other officers joined me with their men, and together we went off to search on our own. We found a magnificent house, quite empty, and here we lodged the men. Some kind of rations had been found. They soon had blazing wood fires going, and seemed happy in a way.

The town major had indicated a hut, where we officers might get rest, and perhaps some food. We went round, tired and aching though we were; we lifted the latch and found ourselves in a glowing room. A stove roared in one corner – and my teeth were chattering with cold, my clothes still being sodden – and a lamp hung from the roof. A large pan of coffee simmered on the stove, and the table was laden with bread, tinned-foods, butter; food, food, food. I hadn't had a bite since early morning, and then not much.

I forget, if I ever knew, who or what the two occupants were, but they were not stragglers. Roye had been their station for some time. One of them was fat, very fat, with a tight, glossy skin. I don't remember the other. We explained that we would like a billet for the night – anything would do so long as it was warmth. They were sorry: they had no room. Could they spare us some rations? They were sorry: this was all they had got till tomorrow noon. We stood very dejected, sick at our reception. 'Come away!' I said. 'Before I go away,' cried one of my companions, 'I would just like to tell these blighters what I think of them.' He cursed them, and then we walked away, back to the men's billet. I looked in at my fellows: most of them were naked, drying their clothes at the fire. Some slept on the floor.

We went upstairs into an empty room. Two of us agreed to make a fire, while the other, the one who had given vent to his feelings, volunteered to go off in search of food. We split up wood we found in the house, and lit a fire. I took off my clothes to dry them, and sat on a bench in my shirt. If I had been asked then what I most desired, besides sleep, I think I would have said: French bread, butter, honey, and hot milky coffee.

The forager soon turned up. God only knows where he got that food from: we did not ask him. But it was French bread, butter, honey, and hot milky coffee in a champagne bottle! We cried out with wonder: we almost wept. We shared the precious stuff out, eating and drinking with inexpressible zest.

As we supped we related our experiences. I forget their names; I don't think I ever knew them. Were they of the Border Regiment? I'm not sure; but they were Northerners. They had been trapped in a sunken road, with a Boche machine-gun at either end, and Boche calling on them to surrender. I don't think either of them was more than twenty years old: they were fresh and boyish, and had been faced with this dilemma. They put it to the vote: there, with death literally staring them in the face, they solemnly called on the men to show hands as to whether they would surrender, or make a run for it. They had voted unanimously for the run. Half of them perished in the attempt. But here, a few hours afterwards, were the survivors, chatting over a blazing wood fire, passing a bottle of coffee round, very unperturbed, not in any way self-conscious. We stacked the fire high and stretched ourselves on the floor in front of it, and slept for a few hours.

IX

We were up at six the next morning, the 26th of March, and reporting to the Assistant Provost-Marshal, who was reorganizing stragglers. We congregated in the Town Square, and I was amazed at the numbers there. The streets were thickly congested with infantrymen from several divisions, with French armoured cars, cavalry, and staff officers. We fell in by divisions, and presently marched off, a column a mile or two in length. Cavalry protected our flanks and rear from surprise.

At Villers-les-Roye I found B\_\_\_\_\_, the man who had been separated from me at Ramecourt Bridge. We were glad to be united again, and from there proceeded together. B\_\_\_\_\_ had had orders to go to a place called La Neuville, where the first-line transport awaited us. We were now passing through the battlefields of 1916, and everywhere was desolate and ruined. We marched on as far as Hangest-en-Santerre, where we met our battalion cookers loaded with a welcome meal. Just as we had devoured this, and were starting on our way again, we were met by a staff colonel, who, after inquiring who we were, ordered us to turn back and proceed to Folies, where our brigade was reorganizing.

We could but mutely obey, but with dull despair and an aching bitterness. We had never thought since leaving Roye but that we were finally out of the mêlée. To turn back meant, we knew, that we might still be very much in it. We crossed country to Folies, about two miles away, in a blazing sun. There we found the details of the brigade, consisting mostly of returned leave men, already holding a line of trenches. We were told to reinforce them.

Here the second-in-command rejoined the battalion and assumed command. My endurance was broken, and I was ordered down to the transport lines. I pointed out that the men were as weary as I, and should on no account be ordered into action again. It was useless: no man could be spared. But there was not much more for them to bear. Good hot food came up to them again at dusk. The night was warm and restful.

On the morning of the 27th, the enemy had possession of Bouchoir, a village about one mile to the south-east. He began to advance during the morning, and a skirmishing fight went on during that day and the next; and during this time the battalion was withdrawn from the line without suffering any serious casualties.

X

But I had gone back with the transport officer on the 26th. I mounted the transport-sergeant's horse, and in a dazed sort of way galloped westward in the dusk. I arrived half-dead at La Neuville, and slept there for twelve hours or more. The next day we went to Braches, and thence on foot to Rouvrel. About here, the country was yet unscathed by war and very beautiful. On a bank by the roadside, I took *Walden* out of my pocket, where it had been forgotten since the morning of the 21st, and there began to read it. At Rouvrel the rest of the battalion rejoined us the next day. On the 29th I set off on horseback with the transport to trek down the valley of the Somme.

When evening came and the hills of Moreuil were faint in the twilight, we were still travelling along the western road. No guns nor any clamour of war could be heard: a great silence filled the cup of misty hills. My weary horse drooped her head as she ambled along, and I, too, was sorrowful. To our north-east lay the squat towers of Amiens, a city in whose defence we had endured hardships until flesh had been defeated, and the brave heart broken. My mind held a vague wonder for her fate – a wonder devoid of hope. I could not believe in the avail of any effort. Then I listened to the rumbling cart, and the quiet voices of the men about me. The first stars were out when we reached Guignemicourt, and there we billeted for the night. In this manner we marched by easy stages down the valley of the Somme, halting finally at Salenelle, a village near Valery, and there we rested four days.

---

*(A) The scheme, common to the Fifth Army, was a defence by distribution in depth. The original front line was reduced to a line of observation posts, from 100 to 500 yards apart, each consisting of a section of men. These men were not intended to resist: they were to observe and give warning to the main line of defence about 200 to 500 yards behind them. This main line was well dug and well wired. But the battalion fronts were extremely long – as long as 2,000 yards – and three companies, perhaps each 100 to 120 strong, became very attenuated along this distance, especially when the men on the observation posts had been deducted. But the line was exceedingly well sited, and, under ordinary circumstances, the machine and Lewis guns, helped by what rifle-fire there was, would have been adequate to cope with any attacking force.

(B) Behind the main line of resistance came the battalion redoubt. This was a circular defensive system, perhaps 800 yards in diameter, manned by the company in battalion reserve, battalion headquarters, and a Machine-Gun Corps unit. The construction of these redoubts was not yet completed, especially in the matter of wiring, and I remember how the colonel used to go round raging about the folly of the man who left his back door undefended.

There was one of these redoubts to each battalion, so that between each redoubt there was a gap of some 1,000 yards. These gaps were covered by machine-guns, and elaborate barrages were worked out by the artillery to cover the approaches to them.

(C) At varying distances behind the front-line system came a second line of redoubts occupied by the brigade in support. These were carefully sited and more or less echeloned with the redoubts 1,000 to 3,000 yards in front. It was one of these redoubts that we occupied at Roupy, and a detailed description of the defence is given in paragraph (F).

(D) Behind this system of redoubts, resting in near villages and camps, came the brigade in reserve. They could be utilized to reinforce or counter-attack any part of the division's frontage.

(E) A line of continuous trenches was in preparation behind the redoubt system, but on our frontage, on the 21st of March, this had only been outlined by removing the sods, and by the construction of one or two machine-gun emplacements. We had only a vague idea of what troops were in Army Reserve, and subsequent experience proved these to be negligible.

(F) The defences we occupied on the morning of the 21st were distributed as follows: the headquarters were in Stanley Redoubt: round this core was the wired ring of the redoubt, occupied on its eastern side by one company. Towards the enemy in front of the redoubt, a short line was occupied by another company detailed to counter-attack should the line in front be broken. This front line was a crescent-shaped irregular line about 1,000 yards long, occupied by two companies. The headquarters of each of these companies was about 200 yards behind the front line in a small keep, wired and defended by a small company-reserve. Communication trenches connected the front-line companies with the counter-attack company, and the counter-attack company with the redoubt. The front-line companies were not well connected with the corresponding companies of the battalion on their flanks. There were gaps which could only be covered by visiting patrols.

The system was, according to British standard, fairly well wired, and the redoubt was well stored with ammunition and reserve water and rations.

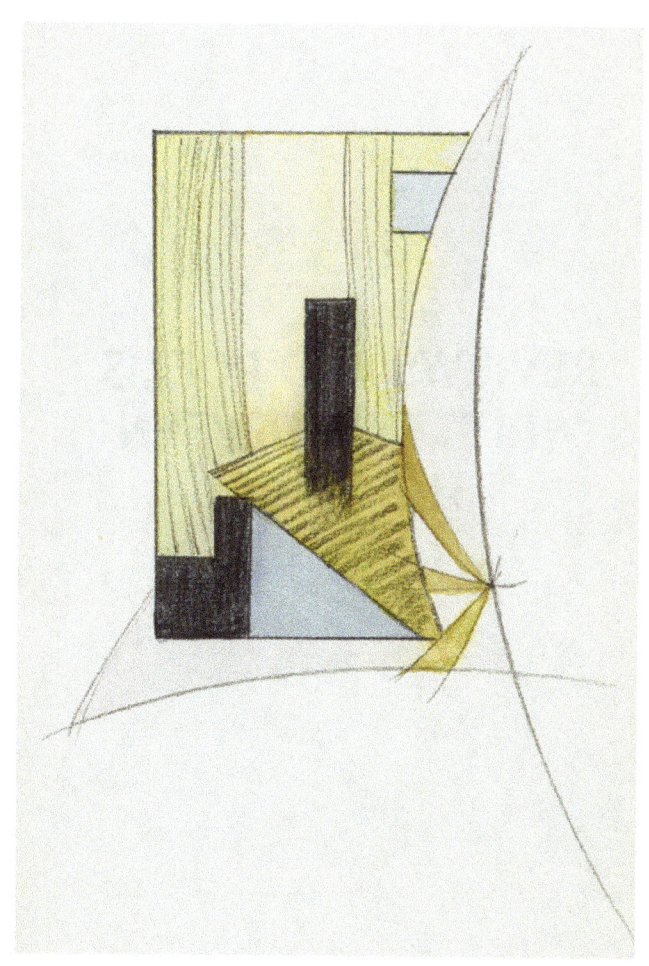

# REVIEWS AND POEMS WRITTEN BETWEEN THE WARS

# A LOST GENERATION

*Review of "All Quiet On The Western Front" by Erich Maria Remarque from "The Nation and Athenaeum" xlv (1929)*

In Germany this book sold 200,000 copies in the first three weeks after publication; by now, not three months after publication, the number of copies sold approaches half a million. And yet it is a severe, masculine book, even a brutal book. It is devoid of romanticism; indeed, it is the negation of romanticism. It cannot be read for pleasure; it is terrible, almost unendurable, in its realism and pathos. But it has swept like a Gospel over Germany, and must sweep over the whole world, because it is the first completely satisfying expression in literature of the greatest event of our time.

I have already, in another periodical, committed myself to the statement that this is the greatest of all war books. I have now read it six or seven times; I have discussed it with men of all degrees, especially with those whose experience of the war was as complete as that of the author; I have tested it faithfully against my own memories; and always my conviction remains firm. I do not deny that there have been other good war books; there have been several, though none so good as the first of all, Barbusse's *Under Fire*. Barbusse was never quite satisfactory because one felt the presence of the humanitarian Socialist; it was realistic enough, but it was also rhetorical, and rhetoric, in this context, was always false. Barbusse, in short, was not universal enough, not detached enough. What did we, in the daily presence of death, care for humanitarian Socialism or any other kind of idealism?

'We' in this context is the generation who spiritually suffered most in the war - the generation who, at the outbreak of war, were under age. It is fr this generation that Remarque specifically speaks. His book is not an indictment of war in the generalized sense; it makes bo accusations, it draws no conclusions. It merely tells the story of a generation of men who, though they may have escaped its shells, were destroyed by the war. For these men, the war lasted too long to be an adventure; it withered something in them that had never come to full growth, something that had never been hardened by the gentler trials of life. It is the seizure of this truth, and the passionate expression of this point of view, that makes Remarque's book so significant:-

> Had we returned home in 1916, out of the suffering and strength of our experiences we might have unleashed a storm. Now if we go back we will be weary, broken, burnt out, rootless, and without hope. We will not be able to find our way any more. And men will not understand us - for the generation that grew up before us, though it has passed these years with us here, already had a home and a calling; now it will return to its old occupations, and the war will be forgotten - and the generation that has grown up after us will be strange to us and push us aside. We will be superfluous even to ourselves, we will grow older, a few will adapt themselves, some others will merely submit, and most will be bewildered; the years will pass by and in the end we shall fall into ruin.

It might seem, that in expressing the point of view of a generation, the author had fallen into the same error as Barbusse, and forgotten that universality which is the essential condition of great art. That is not so, because a man who is 'burnt out' has no prejudices: he is either all or nothing, generally nothing. Hollow men. Why Herr Remarque should rise out of this 'cactus land' and speak so powerfully is perhaps difficult to understand. He himself has stated that it was because there came to him a sudden realization that he alone of all his companions was left alive, and that he alone was left to record their agony. Perhaps in that realization there was a revelation of a greater truth than even this book expresses: that although modern war is wholly devoid of glory, the glory of the human spirit is indestructible, and nowhere was this more evident than in the brutal and degrading experiences of those four terrible years.

This book is the Bible of the common soldier, the Tommy in the front-line who month after month endured the mess and stink of death, and all the loud riot of killing, the testament of the only man who is competent and worthy to speak of the war. When this kind of experience is presented in anger and without art, it only arouses resentment and pity. But this book wins our sympathy by its detachment and by its aesthetic merits. It is a superb piece of construction. It consists of a number of separate scenes and events, varying in tone from the farcical to the tragic, which piece together into a mosaic which has a unity of its own. Each scene is representative of a phase of war experience; at the end of the book it is difficult to think of any significant experience of a man at the front which is not represented: everything is there - horror, coarseness, lewdness, humour, pathos, comradeship, even the unexpected beauty of nature. Gradually death takes toll of it all.

No idealism is left in this generation. We cannot believe in democracy or Socialism, or the League of Nations. To be told at the front that we were fighting to make the world safe for democracy was to be driven to the dumb verge of insanity. On a mutual respect for each other's sufferings we built up that sense of comradeship which was the war's only good gift. But death destroyed even this, and we were left with only the bare desire to live, although life itself was past our comprehension.

# MORE WAR BOOKS
From *The Nation and Athenaeum*, xlvi (1929)

*"German Students' Letters", ed. Dr Philipp Witkop, translated by A. F. Wedd; "Schlump" Anonymous, translated by Maurice Samuel; "Three Personal Records of the War" by R. H. Mottram, John Easton and Eric Partridge; "The West Flanders Plain" by Henry Williamson; "Plain Tales from Flanders" by the Rev. P. B. Clayton.*

War-books are divisible into two kinds, or rather two extremes of perfection. At one extreme is a great work of art, a book which takes war as its theme and treats it in the epic manner; for war with its heroism and sacrifice, its horror and its tragedy, has all the elements of which a great work of art can take shape. Whether the European War has yet produced such a work is a question that it would be idle to discuss: an epic does not spring up in a night, and even if it did, would not be immediately recognized. At the other extreme is the plain record of personal experience. It is a strange fact that this type of war-book is almost as rare as the great epic. Both forms demand for their perfection a suppression of personal feeling that is almost inhuman. The individual, with his prejudices and pettinesses, will keep breaking in.

Between the two extremes this individual point of view finds expression in a mass of impure literature. Most of it, in relation to the war, is pacifist in intention. It has for its object the revelation of the horror and beastliness of war, its utter inhumanity; in that way it hopes to act as a deterrent. But while sympathizing with its aim, one may doubt its efficacy, and precisely in the degree that it satisfies a popular demand, precisely, that is to say, in the degree that it is vivid, moving, even revolting. For the relation of horrors has a peculiar fascination for normal people (even for children, who enjoy the bloodiest fables), and the deterrent effect in relation to the origins of war is absolutely nil. War is made possible (its immediate cause is a different question) by a difference in national modes of feeling and thinking. Without such differences it would be impossible to foment national hatred. The best assurance of peace, therefore, is mutual understanding.

If they are read from this point of view, the war books that crowd upon us can be extraordinarily illuminating. The writers of them, whatever their nationality, have their attention directed to the same object: they are all looking into the same mirror and therefore they meet on the same level. Now when eyes meet in a mirror the effect is always humorous, and though the image is far-fetched, it is worth suggesting that in such a situation the nations of Europe will learn to understand one another.

This batch of books is excellent for the purpose. Two are German in origin, the other three are English. They make illuminating contrasts. The volume of "German Students' Letters" is one of the most valuable war books we have yet seen. It is a selection from a larger collection published earlier in the year in Germany, which collection was in itself a selection from 20,000 letters placed at the disposal of Dr. Witkop through the agency of the German Ministry of Education. This double process of selection may explain a certain uniformity of sentiment common to most of the letters; it may also explain the otherwise curious fact that most of the letters seem to have been written by students killed in the first or second year of the war. The note of bitter disillusionment so frequent in German war books, is scarcely to be found here. Here, instead, is sublime confidence. All the students believe explicitly in the cause they are fighting for, and express themselves with self-conscious righteousness. "Only one thing is real now -- the war! And the only thing that now inspires and uplifts one is love for the German Fatherland and the desire to fight and risk all for Emperor and Empire." How often that cry is repeated in these pages, often with an aspiration to an ideal world to be attained by victory! How different is the English attitude! Mr. Mottram is very English, and this is how he and his kind came into the war: "We had nearly all enlisted in the ranks, and although there must have been great variations , amid so many hundreds of thousands, in the motive, I believe in the main that none of my sort had any military instinct and very little class consciousness. ... I never heard the invasion of Germany mentioned except in joke, and I am quite sure that if we had had any inkling of what the last year of War and first of Peace were to be like, most of us would never have gone, and we would have been an awkward lot to conscript. How were we enlisted? In 1914, so utterly unprepared were we that the dominant note of those days was one of uncomprehending enthusiasm veiled by comedy"

    The English attitude is the more human one, we may modestly claim. It is less the product of education. It is more flexible. Its pitfall is sentimentality.

    The personal records of Mr. Mottram and his bookfellows are some of the best that have appeared; Mr. Mottram's, indeed, is particularly good, avoiding any suggestion of "literary" values, keeping to the facts, without exaggeration and without extenuation. Mr. Williamson's book has previously appeared in a more expensive form, but is reissued after some revision. It is a sensitive work, grounded in disillusion, it is true, but firm in spite of its pathos. It is a retrospective meditation of one who in his disillusionment visits the battlefields of ten years ago, as if to seek there some solace for his bitterness, but in vain. The "Tales" by the Padre-Founder of Toc H are as sentimental as the basis of that institution: Kipling and holy water, they might be called. But the defects are English defects, and to be cured by understanding, not scorn. "Schlump" is a record of a scamp in the war: the kind of man whose energies were mainly devoted to securing cushy jobs, and to the satisfaction of his lusts. It is a curious book, conscienceless, at times unreal. It, too, is a product of disillusionment, but instead of bitterness expresses that far more terrible state of mind, indifference.

# MORE WAR BOOKS
From an unattributed cutting in a scrap book of Herbert Read's published articles at reviews held at the University of Leeds Brotherton Library

*"Class 1902 by Ernst Glaeser; 'German Students' War Letters"; "Schlump", Anonymous; "Zero Hour" by Georg Grabenhorst; "War Bugs" by Charles MacArthur; "Field Guns in France" by Lieut.-Col. Neil Fraser-Tytler; "Fighting Tanks" Edited by C. Murray Wilson; "Plain Tales from Flanders" by the Rev. P. B. Clayton.*

Still the war books pour from the press! Many more are to come. Indeed, we are probably only at the beginning of a period that will last many years, during which those who lived intensely through the war will strive to perpetuate their memories. The event itself was so immense, so shattering, so beyond the the stretch of the normal conception of the mind or imagination that humanity simply recoiled, sick at heart and stunned. Now we begin to recover. Something has been released in our minds, and the world is suddenly eager to confess and to hear confessions. Some people are saying that it will all blow over; the public will soon be bored. The wish is father to the thought. The war is the biggest historical event since the French Revolution: it is infinitely wider in its human reverberations than the French Revolution ever was. Think of the bulk of literature that was born of the French Revolution and multiply it a thousandfold and you will probably have some conception of the literature that will arise out of the suffering and tragedy of the European War. It is useless to turn against a tide that has a world-convulsion as its cause. It is much wiser to flow with it, attempting to keep one's bearings.

The eight books under review are fairly representative of the various types of war-book with which we are confronted. Half of them, and the best half, are translations from the German, and in that respect they are representative, too. There are good war-books being written in England; some have been published, some are in the press, and some are still to be written; but the greatest spiritual values come out of the greatest material suffering, and for this reason Germany has produced, and will continue to produce, the most moving and profound war-books. But even so, this spirit must find individual expression: the occasion must find a poet worthy of it. Pathetic possibilities are revealed in the volume of "German Students' Letters." Young students of philosophy and of theology, of medicine and of law, of chemistry and political economy -- they all speak with the same earnest love of their Fatherland, the same zeal for a new world in which their ideals will be realised. These letters have been selected from some 20,000 placed at the disposal of their editor, Professor Philipp Witkop, and no doubt they represent the cream of the intellectual youth of pre-war Germany. Even so, they are impressive; impressive and a little forbidding. We in England could not produce a volume of the same kind: we do not reason about our actions in the same way. In "Fighting Tanks" there is a vivid narrative of a tank in action by Lieut.-Colonel Elliott Hotbalck, D.S.O., M.C. which throws some light on our shyer mentality. The hero of that narrative at the decisive moment remembers a saying of his brother, a man of few words:

> In life the Great Call comes only once, and when it comes there is every reason why you should not answer it

— every reason but one. If you do answer it, whatever the cost may be, you will kindle a glow of content in your heart that nothing can put out. If you do not answer, it does not matter who else forgives you, you will never forgive yourself.

Some feeling like that was the mainspring of the actions of most Englishmen in the war. It was an instinctive feeling, never rationalised, and capable of degenerating into utter sentimentality -- as it does in some of the modest tales of the Rev. P. B. Clayton, Founder-Padre of Toc H. The German can be sentimental too, in his cumbrous way, for what, after all, can be more sentimental than to deceive oneself with fine sentiments? But at the best he realises, in the words of one of their number, that "what counts is always the readiness to make a sacrifice, not the object for which the sacrifice is made."

There is a realisation of this finer feeling in "Zero Hour," which is a sensitive work, which does not, however, pierce to the reality of war. There is no pretension to anything of the kind in 'Schlump," which is an unblushing study in selfishness and self-complacency. One escape from defeat and disillusion is cynicism: it is a fatalistic attitude adopted by many younger German writers. It is not beautiful, it is not inspiring; but it is generally rooted in experience, and a book like "Schlump" must be read if we want to take account of all the reactions to the war. "Class 1902" represents still another reaction. It shows us the war-mentality of a German schoolboy. It is an extraordinarily sincere psychological study, and easily the best-written book of the batch under review. It represents the point of view of a generation that has not yet been heard --

the generation that grew up in the unhealthy excitement of war, amidst all the horrors, the cynicism, the degredation of all human values, to emerge at the end of their schooldays into a world in ruins. The problems of adolescence, perhaps, bulk unduly in the scene, but then it is so easy for an older man to forget and despise his adolescence. Herr Glaeser was born in 1902, so that impressionable period of life came to him precisely during the years of the war; but for his "class" the war brought no strenuous distraction; it merely intensified the fever in the blood. It is that intensity which makes "Class 1902" a memorable book.

"Field Guns in France" is made up of letters written by an artillery officer in France between November, 1915, and August, 1918. Col. Fraser-Tytler took the business of killing seriously, and does not hesitate to say so. He carried to war all the callous efficiency which a sportsman of his type usually devotes to the shooting of game. Indded he has the effrontery to print as an appendix, and to call it such, a "Gamebook of German Casualties from Personal Observations," totlling "412 Huns." But reprehensible as this attitude of mind is, it is almost noble compared with the disgusting levity of "War Bugs," described by the publishers as "the American version." To treat the war as a tragedy is, perhaps, tiresome; to treat it as a necessary business is, perhaps, unintelligent; but ot treat it as a good joke is merely obscene.

# HISTORY AND REALITY
## from *Time and Tide*, 9 February 1935

*Military Operations -- France and Belgium, 1918: The German March Offensive and its Preliminaries. With Sketches. Compiled by Brigadier-General Sir J. E. Edmonds, C.B., C.M.G.; Separate Volume of Appendices; Separate Case of Maps; all published by Macmillan.*

These volumes cover only six days of the Great War -- 21st to 26th March, 1918 -- but those days were perhaps the most decisive of the whole war on the Western Front. Other actions, Passchendaele on the British Front and Verdun on the French Front -- were more intensive and more terrible; but in the March offensive Germany gathered together her forces for a last desperate fling. If she had succeeded in her objective, which was to break through the line near the junction of the French and British forces and crumple up the British line by outflanking it, the already disintegrating morale of the Germany troops would have been restored, and the future course of the war would have been very different. If Germany failed, she knew she would be ruined. But she did not mean to fail. The withdrawal of Russia from the struggle had freed a large number of divisions; a total of 63, in addition to those already in the line were collected for the assault. Against the 14 divisions of General Gough's Fifth Army they massed no less than 43 divisions. The actual front to be attacked was chosen with great skill. As early as the 16th January General von Sauberzweig, the Chief of the Staff of their Eighteenth Army, had reported:

It may now be accepted that the British have taken over the front of the French III Corps. They will no doubt take over that of the XXXVII Corps up to the Oise, so that in future the Oise will be the boundary between the French and British.

The Eighteenth Army will, therefore, have only British opposite it. This will make the situation more favourable for us.

The offensive is principally intended to strike the British. They now stand opposite to us on the whole front of the Group of Armies which is to make the offensive. It need not be anticipated that the French will run themselves off their legs and hurry at once to the help of their Entente comrades. They will first wait and see if their own front is not attacked also, and decide to support their ally only when the situation has been quite cleared up. That will not be immediately, as demonstrations to deceive the French will be made by the German Crown Prince's Group.

These clever anticipations were all fulfilled. We, on our side, of course, were not without our anticipations, too; and in any case such an immense operation as that contemplated by the Germans could not be prepared without obvious signs. As early as 1st February General Gough reported to General Headquarters that he anticipated an attack on the Fifth Army front, and called attention to the inadequate nature of his forces and supplies. At the same time he pushed forward with all haste a system of defence which made the most effective use of his material. On the 1st February he anticipated that his system of defence would be complete by 15th March. The margin was too narrow for safety, and when the Germans attacked on 21st March, the defences were far from complete. The forward areas, known as the Battle Zone, were reasonably complete, and very skilfully planned. But the main reserve defence line, known as the Green Line, existed mainly on paper; in my sector (XVIII Corps) the sods had been neatly peeled off the ground to show where the line should exist, which was enough to give the German artillery observers a mark to fire at, but utterly useless for cover.

I have already published an account (*In Retreat*) of the part played by an individual unit -- an infantry battalion -- in this six days' battle. It is a short narrative of less than fifty pages. In this history of 550 pages my battalion is mentioned four times, in as many sentences. It is, I suppose, our fair share, and history is a mosaic of "mentions." "An attack on the defences east of Roupy, on the forward edge of the Battle Zone, repulsed by the Second Green Howards at 1.30 p.m., was renewed later, and desperate fighting followed until a late hour." That is the *history* of a day in the lives of several hundred men (the last day in the lives of many of them), a day so vivid and intense that the rest of life has seemed to pivot round it. The history conveys nothing of its reality; and what is true of this one day in the life of one unit, is true of every day and every unit engaged in the war. History does not convey the reality of it. And what is true of this war, is true of all wars, and of all human experience: history does not convey the reality of it. History is a generalization, an abstraction, an aggregation of facts which excludes feeling, excludes humanity, excludes truth. The only truth is in poetry -- in that interpretation of experience which reveals the universal elements in particular events.

But history, though it should not be confused with truth, is a necessary science. Or shall we say that war is a science, whose phenomena must be recorded, for the development of that science. Unfortunately its conditions are unstable, and the lessons to be learned from the last war are not likely to be of much use in another war, should one ever occur. But as a scientific account of objective forces and events, this official history of the war, judging by this section of it, is a very fine performance. An immense number of facts are reduced to connected order; an action taking place over a fifty-mile front is seen as a whole and consecutively followed; and this whole is related to the wider questions of military policy involving the general conduct of the war. The style of narrative is clear and concise, and not unduly technical; sketches and maps are plentiful and well printed. Within the limits set, it is impossible to imagine the work better done.

So far as my own experience of the events goes, the history is very accurate, and most of the comments made are just. The decisive part played by the fog, particularly on the first day of the attack, is rightly emphasized, but the complete breakdown of artillery co-operation is perhaps not stressed sufficiently. The fog partly accounted for this, but the air observation of the Royal Flying Corps was both inadequate and inaccurate; my own battalion was twice shelled out of its position by our own artillery. It is bad enough to be shelled from the front, but at the same time to be shelled from the back produces a terribly demoralizing effect. In commenting on the first day's fighting, General Edmonds is perhaps a little hard on "the men on the spot."

> To British troops, whose instinct is to fight it out where they stand, there came no thought of "elastic yielding," and considerable doubt existed as to whether the garrisons, when the enemy was already in the rear of them, should hold on to the last regardless of what was happening on the right or left.

> Some even of the best new officers did not realize that they must use discretion as being "the men on the spot," and that even orders to hold on may in extreme circumstances be disregarded.

Use our discretion we did; but it was made all the more difficult by the hysterical appeals to hold on to the last man which were the only communications we received from the men not on the spot.

There is one point made by General Edmonds in his Preface that calls for the greatest publicity. It related to the commander of the Fifth Army. "The Army, and particularly his own Army, felt and still feel that as regards events in 1918 he was unfairly treated. This statement is made only after discussion with hundreds of officers, amongst whom there was no dissentient." An enquiry was refused to General Gough, and he is still, in the public mind, under a cloud. The truth is, his reputation was sacrificed to shield the real culprits — the British General Headquarters who did not take his warnings seriously enough, and the French, particularly General Pétain, who completely misjudged the whole situation. Surely it is not too late to honour the General of an Army which, against overwhelming odds, fought and won the decisive battle of the Great War.

# THE FAILURE OF THE WAR BOOKS
*From* News-Letter, iv, 1940

Young writers who took part in the last war came back with one desire: to tell the truth about war, to expose its horrors, its inhumanity, its indignity. They knew that it was no good crying over spilt blood, no good trying to console themselves or their contemporaries. But at least they might warn the coming generations. "All a poet can do to-day is warn," wrote Wilfred Owen. "That is why the true Poets must be truthful."

It took a few years for a new generation to grow up and become war conscious. In the meantime there was no public for war poetry or war stories. Between 1918 and 1928 it was almost impossible to publish anything realistic about war. Then came the reaction. It was slowly mounting when Remarque wrote *All Quiet on the Western Front*. Remarque, like Owen, wanted to warn the new generation. He did warn them; so did the film which was based on his book. So did scores of books that floated to success on the tide of "All Quiet," which itself became the best-selling novel of our time.

At first it looked as though the warning had taken effect. After the spate of anti-war literature, there was the famous debate at the Oxford Union at which an overwhelming majority of undergraduates declared that under no circumstances would they ever take up arms. The Peace Pledge Union sprang into existence and its membership reached hundreds of thousands.

It began to look as though our warning had taken effect, but from the beginning there was something specious about this youthful pacifism. It was based on a negation, whereas a true belief is always positive and affirmative. Further, this negation was the negation of an abstraction -- war. War, thanks to the war books, was vivid enough to the imagination of these young men: it was a nightmare of senseless killing. But war acquires its reality from psychological and economic forces, and it is useless to protest against war unless at the same time there is some understanding of the workings of these primary forces and some attempt to control them.

But there was no such understanding. These forces gathered momentum and now, ten years after the publication of "All Quiet," we are at war again. Our books may have created a few extra conscientious objectors, but in their main purpose, the prevention of another war, they have failed.

In asking the reason for this failure, it is easy to be wise after the event and say that the books were not good enough. It is said of "All Quiet," for example, that it was sentimental. To some extent the criticism is true, but sentimentality was not, for effectiveness, a fault. The nearest parallel to "All Quiet" in the past is *Uncle Tom's Cabin*. That was a much more sentimental book than "All Quiet," yet for that very reason it was largely instrumental in bringing about one of the greatest reforms in the history of mankind -- the abolition of slavery. The abolition of war is no doubt a bigger problem, but if books are to play a part in its solution, they will be books at least as sentimental as "All Quiet."

We must look for a deeper cause of this failure. I believe it can be ascribed to the impulse which is loosely known as sadism, but which is surely something rather broader than that form of sexual perversion. Whatever we call it, there is no doubt that there exists in mankind a love of vicarious suffering and violence. From an early age we delight in stories of strife and bloodshed, and any attempt to eradicate this interest in children only seems to lead to compensatory complexes of a no less disagreeable nature. In writing our war books we were unwittingly ministering to this hidden lust. I have myself been struck by the fact that one and only one of my war poems has been extensively quoted in anthologies and reviews — a simple but very bitter and horrible poem called "The Happy Warrior." From a literary point of view I am sure it is by no means the best of my war poems, but it has had a terrible fascination for many people. It expresses in an extreme degree the horror of war, and it, and other poems and stories of the same kind, should have been an effective warning.

As it is, the suspicion now grows upon me that such writing was fuel to the inner flames of the war spirit. If we human beings have an irresistible urge to destruction, including an urge to self-destruction, then the imagination will feed ravenously on any vivid description of the process of destruction.

Let the poets of this new war realise that they will not prevent a repetition of war by telling the truth. War is not a spirit that can be exorcised by any form of incantation. It is an impulse that must be eradicated by a patient course of treatment.

That treatment will be partly social and partly psychological. That is to say, the necessary psychological treatment cannot take place in the present order of society, that does everything to perpetuate the impulses of competition and power. It can only take place in a society based on the impulses of mutual aid and service — an order of society where all the tendencies are against rivalry and the domination of groups or individuals. If these tendencies, which are by no means against the order of nature, could be established, then we might reasonably hope to eradicate the destructive impulse itself, and to provide adequate alternatives for the expenditure of the latent psychic energies of mankind.

## PROPAGANDA IN PERSPECTIVE

I do not underestimate the power of propaganda, whether in the form of books or periodicals or the spoken word. Once it is in the hands of a single centralised authority, it can mould mass opinion to almost any kind of belief. It can do almost anything short of changing human nature. But it cannot alter the basic instincts of men, and for that reason the uniformity it establishes remains insecure, a façade of stucco without any supporting wall. Human nature can only be changed by environment, genetics and other long-term physical factors. If we want to make mankind a more peace-loving animal, we must first create the right kind of social mould, the right kind of family life, the right kind of education; and all these things must be provided on a world scale, because peace must be universal.

We must continue to tell the truth about war, as about all things. But the telling must be a confession of shame and failure. After this war there must be a new kind of literature. Not a literature of reportage, of pride in experience, of vicarious suffering. But a literature of constructive imagination, of social idealism, of positive morality. To learn by experience -- that is the method of the animal. In so far as we hope to be more than animals we must learn by what is greater than experience -- by experiment.

# THE END OF A WAR (1933)

*'In former days we used to look at life, and sometimes from a distance, at death, and still further removed from us, at eternity. Today it is from afar that we look at life, death is near us, and perhaps nearer still is eternity.'*

- JEAN BOUVIER
a French subaltern, February, 1916

ARGUMENT

*In the early days of November 1918, the Allied Forces had for some days been advancing in pursuit of the retreating German Army. The advance was being carried out according to a schedule. Each division was given a line to which it must attain before night-fall; and this meant that each battalion in a division had to reach a certain point by a certain time. The schedule was in general being well adhered to, but the opposition encountered varied considerably at different points.*

*On November 10<sup>th</sup>, a certain English Battalion had been continuously harassed by machine-gun fire, and late in the afternoon was still far from its objective. Advancing under cover, it reached the edge of a plantation from which stretched a wide open space of cultivated land, with a village in front about 500 years away. The officer in charge of the scouts was sent ahead with a corporal and two men to reconnoitre, and this little party reached the outskirts of the village without observing any signs of occupation. At the entrance of the village, propped against a tree, they found a German officer, wounded severely in the thigh. He was quite* *conscious and looked up calmly as Lieut. S------- approached him. He spoke English and, when questioned, intimated that the village had been evacuated by the Germans two hours ago.*

*Thereupon Lieut. S------- signalled back to the battalion, who then advanced along the road in marching formation. It was nearly dusk when they reached the small place in front of the church, and there they were halted. Immediately from several points, but chiefly from the tower of the church, a number of machine-guns opened fire on the massed men. A wild cry went up, and the men fled in rage and terror to the shelter of the houses, leaving a hundred of their companions and five officers dead or dying on the pavement. In the houses and the church they routed out the ambushed Germans and mercilessly bayoneted them.*

*The corporal who had been with Lieut. S------- ran to the entrance of the village, to settle with the wounded officer who had betrayed them. The German seemed to be expecting him; his face did not flinch as the bayonet descended.*

*When the wounded had been attended to, and the dead gathered together, the remaining men retired to the schoolhouse to rest for the night. The officers then went to the château of the village, and there in a gardener's cottage, searching for fuel, the corporal already mentioned found the naked body of a young girl. Both legs were severed, and one severed arm was found in another room. The body itself was covered with bayonet wounds. When the discovery was reported to Lieut. S--------, he went to verify the strange crime, but there was nothing to be done; he was, moreover, sick and tired. He found a bed in another cottage near the château, where some old peasants were still cowering behind a screen. He fell into a deep sleep, and did not wake until the next morning, the 11th of November, 1918.*

## MEDITATION OF A DYING GERMAN OFFICER

Ich sterbe .... Life ebbs with an easy flow
and I've no anguish now. This failing light
is the world's light: it dies like a lamp
flickering for want of oil. When the last jump comes
and the axe-head blackness slips through flesh
that welcomes it with open but unquivering lips
then I shall be one with the Unknown
this Nothing which Heinrich made his argument
for God's existence: a concept beyond the mind's reach.
But why embody the Unknown: why give to God
anything but essence, intangible, invisible, inert?
The world is full of solid creatures – these
are the mind's material, these we must mould
into images, idols to worship and obey:
The Father and the Flag, and the wide Empire
of our creative hands. I have seen
the heart of Europe send its beating blood
like a blush over the world's pallid sphere
calling it to one life, one order and one living.
For that dream I've given my life and to the last
fought its listless enemies. Now Chaos intervenes
and I leave not gladly but with harsh disdain
a world too strong in folly for the bliss of dreams.

I fought with gladness. When others cursed the day
this stress was loosed
and men were driven into camps, to follow
with wonder, woe, or base delirium
the voiceless yet incessant surge

then I exulted: but with not more
than a nostril's distension, an eager eye
and fast untiring step.

                                                The first week
I crossed the Fatherland, to take my place
in the swift-wing'd swoop that all but ended
the assay in one wild and agile venture.
I was blooded then, but the wound
seared in the burning circlet of my spirit
served only to temper courage
with scorn of action's outcome.
Blooded but not beaten I left the ranks
to be a leader. Four years
I have lived in the ecstasy of battle.
The throbbing of guns, growing yearly,
has been drum music to my ears
the crash of shells the thrill of cymbals
bayonets fiddlers' bows and the crack of rifles
plucked harp strings. Now the silence
is unholy. Death has no deeper horror
than diminishing sound – ears that strain
for the melody of action, hear
only the empty silence of retreating life.
Darkness will be kinder.

                                                                                               I die –
But still I hear a distant gunfire, stirring in my ear
like a weary humming nerve. I will cling to that sound
and on its widening wave

lapse into eternity. Heinrich, are you near?
Best friend, but false to my faith
would you die doubtfully with so calm a gaze?
Mind above battles, does your heart resign
love of the Fatherland in this hour of woe?
No drum will beat in your dying ears, and your God
will meet you with a cold embrace.
The void is icy: your Abstraction
freezes the blood at death: no calm
bound in such a barren law. The bond between
two human hearts is richer. Love can seal
the anguish'd ventricles with subtle fire
and make life end in peace, in love
the love we shared in all this strife.
Heinrich, your God has not this power, or he would heal
the world's wounds and create the empire
now left in the defeated hands of men.

At Valenciennes I saw you turn
swiftly into an open church. I followed
stood in the shadow of the aisle
and watched you pray. My impulse then
was to meet you in the porch and test
my smile against your smile, my peace against yours
and from your abashment pluck a wilder hope.
But the impulse died in the act: your face was blank
drained of sorrow as of joy, and I was dumb
before renunciation's subtler calm.

I let you pass, and into the world went to deny my sight, to
seal my lips

against the witness of your humble faith.
For my faith was action: is action now!
In death I triumph with a deed
and prove my faith against your passive ghost.

Faith in self comes first, from self we build
the web of friendship, from friends to confederates
and so to the State. This web has a weft
in the land we live in, a town, a hill
all that the living eyes traverse. There are lights
given by the tongue we speak, the songs we sing,
the music and the magic of our Fatherland.
This is a tangible trust. To make it secure
against the tempests of inferior minds
to build it in our blood, to make our lives
a tribute to its beauty – there is no higher aim.
This good achieved, then to God we turn
for a crown on our perfection: God we create
in the end of action, not in dreams.

God dies in this dying light. The mists receive
my spent spirit: there is no one to hear
my last wish. Already my thoughts
rebound in a tenement whose doors
are shut: strange muscles clench my jaws
these limbs are numb. I cannot lift
a finger to my will. But the mind
rises like a crystal sphere above the rigid wreck
is poised there, perhaps to fall into the void
still dreaming of an Empire of the West.
And so still feels no fear! Mind triumphs over flesh

ordering the body's action in direst danger.
Courage is not born in men, but born of love
love of life and love of giving, love
of this hour of death, which all love seeks.

I die, but death was destined. My life was given
my death ordained when first my hand
held naked weapons in this war. The rest
has been a waiting for this final hour.
In such glory I could not always live.

My brow falls like a shutter of lead, clashes
on the clench'd jaw. The curtain of flesh
is wreathed about these rigid lines
in folds that have the easy notion of a smile.
So let them kiss earth and acid corruption:
extinction of the clod. The bubble is free
to expand to the world's confines or to break
against the pricking stars. The last lights shine
across its perfect crystal: rare ethereal glimmer
of mind's own intensity. Above the clod
all things are clear, and what is left
is petulant scorn, implanted passions,
everything not tensely ideal. Blind emotions
wreck the image with their blundering wings.
Mind must define before the heart intrigues.


Last night above the world, wavering in the darkest
void of Nothing – how still and tenuous
no music of the spheres – and so break with a sigh

against the ultimate
shores of this world
so finite
so small
Nichts

## DIALOGUE BETWEEN THE BODY AND THE SOUL OF THE MURDERED GIRL

### BODY

I speak not from my pallid lips
but from these wounds.

### SOUL

Red lips that cannot tell
a credible tale.

### BODY

In a world of martyr'd men
these lips renounce their ravage:
The wounds of France
roused their fresh and fluid voices.

### SOUL

War has victims beyond the bands
bonded to slaughter. War moves with armoured wheels
across the quivering flesh and patient limbs
of all life's labile fronds.

### BODY

France was the garden I lived in.
Amid these trees, these fields, petals fell

flesh to flesh; I was a wilder flower.

SOUL

Open and innocent. So is the heart
laid virgin to my choice. I filled
your vacant ventricles with dreams
with immortal hopes and aspirations that exalt
the flesh to passion, to love and hate.
Child-radiance then is clouded, the light
that floods the mind is hot with blood
pulse beats to the vibrant battle-cry
the limbs are burnt with action.

BODY

The heart had not lost its innocence so soon
but for the coming of that day when men
speaking a strange tongue, wearing strange clothes
armed, flashing with harness and spurs
carrying rifles, lances or spears
followed by rumbling wagons, shrouded guns
passed through the village in endless procession
swift, grim, scornful, exulting.

SOUL

You had not lost your innocence so soon
but for the going of men from the village
your father gone, your brother
only the old left, and the very young

the women sad, the houses shuttered
suspense of school, even of play
the eager search for news, the air
of universal doubt, and then the knowledge
that the wavering line of battle now was fixed
beyond this home. The soil was tilled
for visionary hate.

BODY

Four years was time enough
for such a seedling hate to grow
sullen, close, intent;
To wait and wonder
but to abate
no fervour in the slow passage of despair.

SOUL

The mind grew tense.

BODY

My wild flesh was caught
in the cog and gear of hate.

SOUL

I lay coiled, the spring
of all your intricate design.

BODY

You served me well. But still I swear
Christ was my only King.

SOUL

France was your Motherland:
To her you gave your life and limbs.

BODY

I gave these hands and gave these arms
I gave my head of ravelled hair.

SOUL

You gave your sweet round breasts
like Agatha who was your Saint.

BODY

Mary Aegyptiaca
is the pattern of my greatest loss.

SOUL

To whom in nakedness and want
God sent a holy man.
Who clothed her, shrived her, gave her peace
before her spirit left the earth.

BODY

My sacrifice was made to gain
the secrets of these hostile men.

SOUL

I hover round your fameless features
barred from Heaven by light electric.

BODY

All men who find these mauled remains
will pray to Mary for your swift release.

SOUL

The cry that left your dying lips
was heard by God.

BODY

I died for France.

SOUL

A bright mantle fell across your bleeding limbs.
Your face averted shone with sacred fire.
So be content. In this war
many men have perished not bless'd
with faith in a cause, a country or a God
not less martyrs than Herod's Victims, Ursula's Virgins

or any mass'd innocents massacred.

                             BODY

Such men give themselves not to their God but to their fate
die thinking the face of God not love but hate.

                             SOUL

Those who die for a cause die comforted and coy;
believing their cause God's cause they die with joy.

## MEDITATION OF THE WAKING ENGLISH OFFICER

I wake: I am alive: there is a bell
sounding with the dream's retreating surf
O catch the lacey hem dissolv'd in light
that creeps along the healing tendrils of a mind
still drugg'd with sleep. Why must my day
kill my dreams? Days of hate. But yes a bell
beats really on this air, a mad bell.
The peasants stir behind that screen.
Listen: they mutter now: they sing
in their old crackt voices, intone
a litany. There are no guns
only these voices of thanksgiving. Can it be?
Yes yes yes: it is peace, peace!
The world is very still, and I am alive!
Alive, alive, alive ...
O limbs, your white radiance
no longer to stand against bloody shot
this heart secure, to live and worship
to go God's way, to grow in faith
to fight with and not against the will!
That day has come at last! Suspended life
renews its rhythmic beat. I live!
Now can I love and strive, as I have dreamt.

Lie still, and let this litany
of simple voices and the jubilant bell
ease rebirth. First there are the dead to bury
O God, the dead. How can God's bell
ring out from that unholy ambush?

That tower of death! In excess of horror
war died. The nerve was broken
fray'd men fought obscenely then: there was no fair joy
no glory in the strife, no blessed wrath.
Man's mind cannot excel
mechanic might except in savage sin.
Our broken bodies oiled the engines: mind was grit.

Shall I regret my pact? Envy that friend
who risked ignominy, insult, gaol
rather than stain his hands with human blood?
And left his fellow men. Such lonely pride
was never mine. I answered no call
there was no call to answer. I felt no hate
only the anguish of an unknown fate
a shot, a cry: then armies on the move
the sudden lull in daily life
all eyes wide with wonder, past surprise:
our felt dependence on a ruling few:
the world madness: the wild plunge:
the avalanche and I myself a twig
torn from its mother soil
and to the chaos rendered.
     Listless
I felt the storm about me; its force
too strong to beat against; in its swirl
I spread my sapling arms, toss'd on its swell
I rose, I ran, I down the dark world sped
till death fell round me like a rain of steel
and hope and faith and love coiled in my inmost cell.

Often in the weariness of watching
warding weary men, pitch'd against
the unmeaning blackness of the night, the wet fog,
the enemy blanketed in mystery, often
I have questioned my life's inconstant drift;
God not real, hate not real, the hearts of men
insentient engines pumping blood
into a spongy mass that cannot move
above the indignity of inflicted death:
the only answer this: the infinite is all
and I, a finite speck, no essence even
of the life that falls like dew
from the spirit breathed on the fine edge
of matter, perhaps only that edge
a ridge between eternal death and life eternal
a moment of time, temporal.
The universe swaying between Nothing and Being
and life faltering like a clock's tick
between a pendulum's coming and going.
The individual lost: seventy years
seventy minutes, have no meaning.
Let death, I cried, come from the forward guns
let death come this moment, swift and crackling
tick-tock, tick-tock – moments that pass
not reckoned in the infinite.

Then I have said: all is that must be.
There is no volition, even prayer
dies on lips compress'd in fear.
Where all must be, there is no God
for God can only be the God of prayer

an infinitely kind Father whose will
can mould the world, who can
in answer to my prayer, mould me.
But whilst I cannot pray, I can't believe
But in this frame of machine necessity
must renounce not only God, but self.
For what is the self without God?
A moment not reckoned in the infinite.
My soul is less than nothing, lost,
unless in this life it can build
a bridge to life eternal.

In a warm room, by the flickering fire
in friendly debate, in some remote
shelter'd existence, even in the hermit's cell
easy it is to believe in God: extend the self
to communion with the infinite, the eternal.
But haggard in the face of death
deprived of all earthly comfort, all hope of life,
the soul a distill'd essence, held
in a shaking cup, spilt
by a spit of lead, saved
by chance alone
very real
in its silky bag of skin, its bond of bone,
so little and so limited,
there's no extenuation then.
Fate is in facts: the only hope
an unknown chance.

So I have won through. What now?

Will faith rise triumphant from the wreck
despair once more evaded in a bold
assertion of the self: self to God related
self in God attain'd, self a segment
of the eternal circle, the wheel
of Heaven, which through the dust of days
and stagnant darkness steadily revolves?

Your gentian eyes stared from the cold
impassive alp of death. You betrayed us
at the last hour of the last day
a smile your only comment
on the well-done deed. What mind
have you carried over the confines?
Your fair face was noble of its kind
some visionary purpose cut the lines
clearly on that countenance.
But you are defeated: once again
the meek inherit the kingdom of God.
No might can win against this wandering
wavering grace of humble men.
You die, in all your power and pride:
I live, in my meekness justified.

When first this fury caught us, then
I vowed devotion to the rights of men
would fight for peace once it came again
from this unwilled war pass gallantly
to wars of will and justice.
That was before I had faced death
day in day out, before hope had sunk

to a little pool of bitterness.
Now I see, either the world is mechanic force
and this the last tragic act, portending
endless hate and blind reversion
back to the tents and healthy lusts

of animal men: or we act
God's purpose in an obscure way.
Evil can only to the Reason stand
in scheme or scope beyond the human mind.
God seeks the perfect man, plann'd
to love him as a friend: our savage fate
a fire to burn our dross
to temper us to finer stock
man emerging in some inconceived span
as something more than remnant of a dream.

To that end worship God, join the voices
heard by these waking ears. God is love:
in his will the meek heart rejoices
doubting till the final grace a dove
from Heaven descends and wakes the mind
in light above the light of human kind
in light celestial
infinite and still
eternal
bright

**The following note was placed at the end of the first and all subsequent printings of *The End of a War*:**

*'It was necessary for my poetic purpose to take an incident from the War of 1914-18 which would serve as a focus for feelings and sentiments otherwise diffuse. The incident is true, and can be vouched for by several witnesses still living. But its horrors do not accuse any particular nation; they are representative of war and of human nature in war. It is not my business as a Poet to condemn war (or, to be more exact, modern warfare). I only wish to present the universal aspects of a particular event. Judgment may follow, but should never precede or become embroiled with the act of poetry. It is for this reason that Milton's attitude to his Satan has so often been misunderstood.'*

# THE SPANISH CIVIL WAR

## BOMBING CASUALTIES IN SPAIN

Dolls' faces are rosier but these were children
their eyes not glass but gleaming gristle
dark lenses in whose quicksilvery glances
the sunlight quivered. These blench'd lips
were warm once and bright with blood
but blood
held in a moist bleb of flesh
not spilt and spatter'd in tousled hair.

In these shadowy tresses
red petals did not always
thus clot and blacken to a scar.
These are dead faces.
Wasps' nests are not so wanly waxen
Wood embers not so greyly ashen.

They are laid out in ranks
like paper lanterns that have fallen
after a night of riot
extinct in the dry morning air.

## THE HEART CONSCRIPTED

The shock of silver tassels
the sledded breath ...
I who have fought my battles
keep these in a sheath.

The ulcer of exact remorse
from which the Lake poet perished,
the owl's indifferent hood –
these have vanished.

I hear only the sobbing fall
of various water-clocks
and the swift inveterate wail
of the destructive axe.

Lorca was killed, singing,
and Fox who was my friend.
The rhythm returns: the song
which has no end.

# LAMENT FOR SPAIN
## From *Spain and the World*, December 1938

We are the victims of a trance that stay
In England's April bower this fateful year.
Our eyes are filled with drowsy light: a warm breath
Drifts gently over the withered fields. Upon the hills
The cherry-orchards lie like fallen clouds
Through which the sun has poured its tranquil gold.
Bright with firstling flowers my garden mocks

The dungeoned spirit brooding in its midst.
Among the birds that fill the virgin dusk
With plaintive songs, one voice that was not heard
Since love and longing ceased under the summer sun
Drops into the chilling air its vivid notes.
The nightingale is here again: he sits

On the same bough of the self-same tree
Where year by year with scarce a day's delay
He keeps his tryst. Down all the vale
Where oak trees rise above the ragged hedge
His fellow migrants take their stand, and as the stars
Throb into sight above the leafless elms.
Their songs, which faltered for a while,
Swell into a loud and sequent threnody.

Hither as he winged his way, this bird
Rested in some Iberian grove and saw
Tangled like the olive roots the limbs of men

Fallen that day defending Spain.
In the abandon of death they had embraced
Earth or sky: the silver light revealed
Cords of blood across their naked breasts.
They were a remnant band that stranded here
Fought till their last shot was gone,
Then met the armoured horde with lifted fist
And the cry of their faith: *No pasarán!*

    Their bodies stiffen in the upland air.
    The night is not still, guns and limbers
    Rumble on the distant road; a burning house
    Wounds with its ruddy glow the dove-soft sky
    And moaning women search the ruined fields.

Like the shadow of a falling leaf you flitted
Through the intricate thickets of death.
Your spirit was driven to seek
A cool nest in the north. You did not sing
Over these sombre men; but you caught as you passed
A sobbing note, and now when you sing
In an English valley, your passionate song
Is no longer serene. Symbol of love and life
It fills this April night with a wild lament.

# NEARER TO REALITY
## From *Revolt*, 11 February 1939

The year has opened tragically for the true friends of Spain, but the disasters which have filled us with sorrow and apprehension can also serve to bring us nearer to reality. It is not that we have been living in a fool's paradise, there is nothing, either in the history of our movement or in the present alignment of forces, that could for a moment lead us to suppose that freedom and justice were easy to uphold. It is doubtful if our cause can ever be established by force of arms, because the arms we bear are dangerous, even to ourselves. The instruments of death are incompatible with freedom. We fervently desire the victory of the Spanish people and with victory we hope to carry forward our libertarian policy. A victory for Franco would mean, instead of an open campaign for freedom, for federalism and for workers' control, a return to the dark battle against tyranny. We do not fear that prospect. We know that though we are without wealth and opportunity to buy the weapons of modern warfare, we fight with the irresistible armament of our ideals. Against us is an embodiment of force and might – a power that must perish of its spiritual and intellectual poverty; with us is the immortal flame of humanity – the truth and love which penetrate all barriers and bring us, through centuries of oppression, nearer to the good life.

The mighty armaments which Franco has secured from his fascist allies may subdue the Spanish people, but they cannot extinguish the knowledge and enlightenment which have come into their lives. Indeed, the effect of this long strife is quite the contrary. It has illuminated, as never before, the misery of a people; it has thrown into sharp opposition the ideals of freedom and of force; it has caused millions of simple people, who never before dared to lift their minds above the dull routine of their slavish lives, to question the justice of their lot and to yearn for a fairer existence. The ideas which we had to instil by propaganda and education are now a common possession of all the people; and once a people is roused to a consciousness of its rights, once love replaces duty in their hearts, and mutual aid is seen as an alternative to moral and economic servitude, then no power of armaments and no alien mercenaries can for long withstand the spiritual power that is generated in their midst.

The Spanish tragedy brings us nearer to reality – above all to the realisation that the international solidarity of the working classes, which is the only force we can oppose to capitalism and fascism, does not yet exist. Do not let us disguise the ugly truth: the Spanish workers have been betrayed by their British, French and American comrades. History will record to our shame that in these very years which saw the destruction of the Spanish democracy for want of arms, our own workers were busily engaged on the rearmament of their capitalist masters.

We must create new bonds of international solidarity, free from the weaknesses inherent in parliamentary socialism. We must return to the foundations of our faith, for it is the head of this giant democracy, and not the feet, that has proved to be made of traitorous clay.

Our immediate duty is to alleviate our guilt with acts of solidarity. A people, homeless and persecuted because of the faith they share with us, must be rescued from death and despair. We must stir the conscience of our country, so that it gives shelter and food to those who are destitute because we have refused them arms for their self-defence.

# THE PRE-REQUISITE OF PEACE
from *Poetry and Anarchism*, 1938

War is a cancer that threatens to destroy the life of our civilisation, but I doubt if any direct surgery will remove it. It's symptoms are obvious, but its causes are secret, deeply buried in the history and habits of our body which bears it. The problem is not so easy to solve as most of our pacifists assume. It may be that there is an abstract ethical question, and about the answer is unequivocally in favour of universal peace. It may be that there is a concrete biological question, and that the answer is as unequivocally in favour of war. I doubt very much whether all the answers to all the questions that can be raised on this issue can be unanimous. There is not only a conflict of values involved, but also a hopeless confusion of motives. Some of the most aggressive and egotistical people I know are active pacifists; some of the gentlest and most sensitive men I have ever met were professional soldiers. They, too, hated war; but they accepted it.

I do not accept war. I consider that it is an insult to the life of reason; that it is cruel and senseless and wholly evil in its effects. Of its economic and social consequences I do not proposed to speak: it is surely obvious enough to all who have lived in the post-war Epoque but these have been disastrous. I seem to remember that Mr Douglas Jerald once maintained that the great war had been worthwhile because it had achieved the westernisation of Turkey, but most of us find it hard to believe that the abolition of the harem and the fez was worth the sacrifice of 12 million lives.

In my opinion, the most convincing arguments for war are not logical at all, but based on certain obscure psychological motives. I do not mean that the arguments are convincing because they are obscure (a not unknown state of affairs). I mean that certain rationalisations of war persist because they are the expression of an emotional energy which would otherwise be repressed. When these rationalisations take a definite and elaborate form, the process of sublimation is obvious enough to anyone with a psychological training. But it is more difficult to explain a far more general attitude towards War and peace which is not active opposition or defence, that uncertainty and apathy. There may be 200,000 active pacifists in Great Britain; there are a few thousand active militarists; but the millions who will be decimated in the next war remain in the Mass indifferent to the fate which threatens them, as sullen as gunpowder before it is fired.

I do not underestimate the important psychological factors which disposers the individual and the nation to a state of war mindedness. But the psychology of man kind is not unalterable: it is on the contrary the most fluent and adaptable aspect of human life. We are at the mercy of unconscious forces, but what is unconscious now can be analysed and brought to the surface; we can discover the physical and material elements which cause or condition these unconscious forces; and by controlling these basic elements we can eventually change the mental life of mankind. This mental life has changed often in the past, but only haphazardly and irrationally; we need the knowledge and resolution to change it deliberately and reasonably.

The only immediately realistic approach to the problem of war is economic. Economic imperialism is so demonstrably dependent on the support of armed force that only the most prejudiced capitalist can pretend to ignore its importance as a factor in the encouragement of warlike instincts. But the capitalist is quite logical (and for once he has the support of the psychologist) when he points out that warfare has a longer history than capitalism, and that the establishment of socialism in Russia, for example, has by no means being accompanied by the decline of the martial spirit. It may be argued that the militarism of the USSR is purely defensive; but it is militarism non-the less, and there are few countries in the world where the pacifist is less free to preach his gospel of nonresistance. So long as nationalism persists as a sentiment, so long as collectivism masquerades as socialism, so long will socialist units be nothing more than capitalist units writ large.

War increases in intensity and effect as a society develops in group organisation. The greatest intensification of the horrors of war is a direct result of the democratisation of the state. So long as the army was a professional unit, the specialist function of a limited number of men, so long war remained a relatively harmless contest for power. But once it became every man's duty to defend his home (or his political 'rights') warfare was free to range wherever that home might be, and to attack every form of life and property associated with that home.

The economic foundations of peace will never be secure so long as the national boundaries exist; they will never be secure so long as collective units such as the nation to exist. So long as it is possible to unite men in the name of an abstraction, war will exist; for the possibility of uniting the whole of mankind under the same abstraction is too to be worth considering, and so long as two or more abstractions exist with collective forces organised behind them, the possibility of war will exist.

The only pacifist peoples are certain so-called savage tribes living under a system of communal land tenure in a land of plenty: communities where are the accumulation of capital and the power it gives has no purpose and therefore does not exist, and where there is no possibility of one-man exploiting the labour of another. These conditions create not only the social and economic possibilities of peace, but also the much more important psychological possibilities. Such communities are, in the precise meaning of the word, anarchist communities.

There is no problem to which, during the last 20 years, I have given more thought than this problem of War and peace. There is no problem which leads so inevitably to anarchism. Peace is anarchy. Government is force; force is repression, and repression leads to reaction, to a psychosis of power, which in its turn involves the individual in destructive impulses and the nations in war. War, therefore, will exist so long as the state exists. Only a non-governmental society can offer those economic, ethical and psychological conditions under which the emergence of a pacifist mentality is possible. We fight because we are too tightly swathed in bonds - because we live in a condition of economic slavery and of moral inhibition. Not until these bonds are loosed will the desire to create finally triumph over the desire to destroy. We must be at peace with ourselves before we can be at peace with one another.

# SECOND WORLD WAR POEMS

## LOGOS

Suddenly he began to torture the flowers
began to twist red winter tulips
faced by the behemothian jaws
for which there is no inevitable IN and OUT

The carnage at the Menin Gate
the startled blackcock's raucous cry
the Morse code of a boot and crutch
filled the space between river and sky.

But stay! The light is cancelled there
the dark eyes cease
to stare at suns
and light breaks in behind the brain.

## TO A CONSCRIPT OF 1940

> *Qui n'a pas une fois désesperé de l'honneur,*
> *ne sera jamais un héros.*
> — George Bernanos

A soldier passed me in the freshly fallen snow
His footsteps muffled, his face unearthly gray;
And my heart gave a sudden leap
As I gazed on a ghost of five-and-twenty years ago.

I shouted Halt! and my voice had the old accustom'd ring
And he obeyed it as it was obeyed
In the shrouded days when I too was one
Of an army of young men marching

Into the unknown. He turned towards me and I said:
'I am one of those who went before you
Five-and-twenty years ago: one of the many who
    never returned,
Of the many who returned and yet were dead.

We went where you are going, into the rain and the mud;
We fought as you will fight
With death and darkness and despair;
We gave what you will give – our brains and our blood.

We think we gave in vain. The world was not renewed.
There was hope in the homestead and anger in the streets
But the old world was restored and we returned
To the dreary field and workshop, and the immemorial feud

Of rich and poor. Our victory was our defeat.
Power was retained where power had been misused
And youth was left to sweep away
The ashes that the fires had strewn beneath our feet.

But one thing we learned: there is no glory in the deed
Until the soldier wears a badge of tarnish'd braid;
There are heroes who have heard the rally and have seen
The glitter of a garland round their head.

Theirs is the hollow victory. They are deceived.
But you, my brother and my ghost, if you can go
Knowing that there is no reward, no certain use
In all your sacrifice, then honour is reprieved.

To fight without hope is to fight with grace,
The self reconstructed, the false heart repaired.'
Then I turned with a smile, and he answered my salute
As he stood against the fretted hedge, which was like
    white lace.

## ODE
*Written during the battle of Dunkirk, May, 1940*

1

Fair now this world of peace
this May sun rising over the quicken'd birds
giving the tender leaves
a human warmth: opening
with golden fingers the heart of the rose.

Gently, ceaselessly, the fretted oaks
sway against the sky: not a bough or leaf
is still. The slender grasses
shiver in urgent freshness.

A butterfly desperately clings
to the shaking bell of a hyacinth.
On the sunned earth
an Iceland poppy has shed its petals
they shrivel in the heat
soon to disintegrate
cell by cell
in the slow material
kiss of death.

The same sun once sucked the film
out of the fallen seed: the mastic phlegm
flooded the dry fibre: there was life
and growth, colour and form. There was man
a coral plasm clinging to shafts of bone

fragile flesh that will fall
like a petal on the provident soil.

The mystery could end there
in birth and death, in wax and wane
and in all that for the interim
dazzles the world with bloom.

But just as the cool luminous clouds
inexplicably thicken in the clear air
to drift across the sun like ragged clots
spreading darkness over the green and eminent land
so there rises in the flesh of man
a forest lust: the rosy fanes
are flush'd with a darker blood: the human bond
is broken, the race divided. The petals
no longer lie withering where they fall
but are torn and crush'd, and into the soil
mashed rawly.

2

The old guns
barked into my ear. Day and night
they shook the earth in which I cowered
or rained around me
detonations of steel and fire.

One of the dazed and disinherited
I crawled out of that mess
with two medals and a gift of blood-money.

No visible wounds to lick – only a resolve
to tell the truth without rhetoric
the truth about war and about men
involved in the indignities of war.

But the world was tired and would forget
forget the pain and squalor
forget the hunger and dread
forget the cry of those who died in agony
and the unbearable silence of those who suddenly
as we talked
fell sniped
with mouth still open and uncomprehending eyes.

It is right to forget
sights the mind cannot accommodate
terror that cannot be described
experience that cannot be exorcised in thought.

It is natural for others to resent
the parade of wounds
eyes haunted with unrevealed sorrows
the unholy pride of sacrifice.

Human to relapse
into the old ways, to resume
the normality so patiently acquired
in days of peace.

And so we drifted twenty years
down the stream of time

feeling that such a storm
could not break again.

Feeling that our little house-boat was safe
until the last lock was reached.
Another twenty years
would see us home.

The day passes
the sun swerves
silently like a cyclist round the bend.
Disembodied voices drift past behind the hedge
the vespers of the blackbird and the thrush
rise and die. A golden frog
leaps out of the grasses.

In the silence of the twilight
I hear in the distance
the new guns.
I listen, no longer apt in war
unable to distinguish between bombs and shells.

As the evening deepens
searchlights begin to waver in the sky
the airplanes throb invisibly above me.
There is still a glow in the west
and Venus shines brightly over the wooded hill.

Unreal war! No single friend
links me with its immediacy.
It is a voice out of a cabinet

a printed sheet, and these faint reverberations
selected in the silence
by my attentive ear.

Presently I shall sleep
and sink into deeper oblivion.

3

Belief without action
action without thought
the blind intervention
of years without design.

We have known that a certain way of life was good
the easy salutation, the open hand
the sober disquisition, the frank eye
the unfailing satisfaction
of water wine and bread.

A step as measur'd
as a sower's on the field
quiet voices, voices of children
benedictions of women, ministrations
of gentle fingers
a centre to the circle
of all our wanderings.
And from this centre
the mind leaving the placid body
freely to range in thought and fantasy.

The world our person
the self the nucleus
the inner kernel round which
the films and shells are wrapt
deceptive or protective.

Our person our world
flex'd limbs, elastic muscles
flow and flood, ripple of breath and blood
against the skeleton's brittle wall
eye's eagerness, lickerous tongue
ear's selection, finger's fine division
all senses single and combin'd
construing the living scene
extending and contracting
finding
the livid elements the languorous the sublime.

These elements accepted but not guarded
faith formulated but not maintain'd
twenty years
without design.

4

This is the hour of retribution
the city shaken, the power taken
from palsied hands.

This is the hour of retribution
the last farewell and the repetition

of the father's sacrifice.

This is the hour of retribution
of power without pity, of work without reward
of poetry without rhetoric.

This is the hour of retribution
the sense of glory kindled, dwindling in the steel cabin
chok'd with burnt petrol.

This is the hour of retribution
the leap from earth, ecstasy in the air
the quickly withering nerve.

This is the hour of retribution
for young men in uniform, for old men in slacks
for children at play.

This is the hour of retribution
the hour of doom, the hour of extreme unction
the hour of death.

5

Happy are those who can relieve
suffering with prayer
Happy those who can rely on God
to see them through.

They can wait patiently for the end.

But we who have put our faith

in the goodness of man
and now see man's image debas'd
lower than the wolf or the hog –

Where can we turn for consolation?

6

The forts have all been taken and the last river cross'd
our cities have fallen our defenders are dead
now we must have faith in the children of the nations
and in Time which for the tyrant is a talisman of dread.

He has put down a people but the people will rise again
like water living water rising through the sand.
He has destroy'd their poets their seers and imagemakers but
others will be born and their works will withstand
the advance of armies that have power but no grace
the peril of persecution and sudden secret death
dispersion and destruction fire and brute burial.
For against his symbol is the spirit and the spirit is a breath

that rises invincible to seek reincarnation
in flesh that cannot be defeated in hearts that rescind
the powers without persuasion the hands without art
to reign in aeons that are ageless in worlds without end.

7

Persevere through despair.
If in danger

faith is maintain'd
the instruments of attainment
form in a furnace
fiercer than war.

The self, passively receiving
illusion and despair
excluding
the unreal power of symbols
the false shelter of institutions
returns reluctantly upon its self
grows like a bud
petal by petal
exfoliated from an infinite centre
the outer layers bursting and withering
the inner pressure increasing
seeking the light
and the flush of colour born of light.

The root deep in the dark soil of the past
but deeper in the unform'd future
is folded the flower.
The sun
has a hot dry breath.

8

Shield the shoot
interpose a misty veil
water the root
this flower shall exhale

its scented peace
bringing to the war-weary world
the perennial release
from fear.

The self perfected
tranquil as a dove
the heart elected
to mutual aid.

Reason and love
incurv'd like a prow
a blade dividing
time's contrary flow.

Poetry a pennon
rippling above
in the fabulous wind.

## WAR AND PEACE

The kind of war is chang'd: the crusade heart
out-shatter'd : flesh a stain on broken earth
and death an unresisted rain.

The horror loos'd all honour is lost.
Peace has pride and passion: but no evil
to equal the indignity of war, whose ringing anvil
wins only anguish. The weighted hammer
breaks the stretch'd tendons at the wrist

And leaves the soul a twisted nail
tearing the flesh that still would live
and give to words the brutal edge of truth.

## THE CONTRARY EXPERIENCE

### 1

You cry as the gull cries
dipping low where the tide has ebbed
over the vapid reaches: your impulse
died in the second summer of the war.

The years dip their boughs
brokenly over the uncovered springs.
Hands wasted for love and poetry
finger the hostile gunmetal.

Called to meaningless action
you hesitate
meditating faith to a conscience
more patently noble.

### 2

But even as you wait
like Arjuna in his chariot
the ancient wisdom whispers:
Live in action.

I do not forget the oath
taken one frosty dawn
when the shadows stretched
from horizon to horizon:

Not to repeat the false act
not to inflict pain:
To suffer, to hope, to build
to analyse the indulgent heart.

Wounds dried like sealing-wax
upon that bond
But time has broken
the proud mind.

No resolve can defeat suffering
no desire establish joy:
Beyond joy and suffering
is the equable heart

not indifferent to glory
if it lead to death
seeking death
if it lead to the only life.

3

Lybia, Egypt, Hellas
the same tide ebbing, the same gull crying
desolate shores and rocky deserts
hunger, thirst, death

the storm threatening and the air still
but other wings
librating in the ominous hush
and the ethereal voice

thrilling and clear.

Buffeted against the storm's sullen breath
the lark rises
over the grey dried grasses
rises and sings.

## A WORLD WITHIN A WAR

*L'espérance est le seul bien que le dégoût respecte*

- Vauvenargues

### 1

Sixteen years ago I built this house
By an oak tree on an acre of wild land
Its walls white against the beechwood
Its roof of Norfolk reed and sedge.

The mossy turf I levelled for a lawn
But for the most part left the acre wild
Knowing I could never live
From its stony soil. My work is within
Between three stacks of books. My window
Looks out on a long line of elms.

A secular and insecure retreat –
The alien world is never far away.
Over the ridge, beyond the elms
The railway runs: a passing train
Sends a faint tremor through the ground
Enough to sever a rotted picture-cord
Or rattle the teaspoon against my cup.
A dozen times a day a red bus
Trundles down the lane: there is the screech and scuttle
Of minor traffic: voices rise
Suddenly from silent wheels.

But such dusty veins drain the land
And leave an interstitial stillness.

The hedgehog and the grass-snake
Still haunt my wood. Winter
Brings the starv'd wildlings nearer: once
We woke to find a fox's tracks
Printed on the crisp film of snow.
It was the first year of my second war
When every night a madden'd yaffle
Thrummed on the icicled thatch.
Another day a reckless kestrel
Dashed against a gable and fell
Dead at my feet: the children
Watched its dying flutter and the fiery eye
Slowly eclips'd under a dim grey lid.

For years the city like a stream of lava
Crept towards us: now its flow
Is frozen in fear. To the sere earth
The ancient ritual returns: the months
Have their heralidic labours once again.
A tractor chugs through frozen clods
And gold buds bead the gorse
In coppices where besom-heads are cut.
Hedges are trimm'd again and primroses
Bunched in splendour on the open banks.
The sparring rooks pick twigs
For shockhead nests built high
In the dark tracery of the elms.
April and the nightingales will come

From an alien world. The squirrels
Chatter in the green hazel-trees.
The nuthatch inspects the oak's ribb'd bark
While the robin jumps round his own domain.
The hay is mown in June. With summer
Comes all ripeness, rusty, red and gold
To die in September. The reaper
Spirals round the blanch'd fields
The corn diminishing until at last
The expected moment comes and rabbits
Zigzag across the glistening stubble
Pursued by yelping dogs and sudden guns.
In December the corn is thresh'd:
In the frosty evening the engine's smoke
Trails slowly above the berried twigs
And meets the rising mist.

2

Sedate within this palisade
Which unforethinking I have made

Of brittle leaves and velvet flowers,
I re-indite a Book of Hours

Would emulate the Lombard School
(Crisp as medals, bright but cool)

Talk mainly of the Human Passion
That made us in a conscious fashion

Strive to control our human fate:
But in the margins interpolate

Apes and angels playing tunes
On harpsichords or saxophones

Throughout the story thus maintain
Under a sacred melody the bass profane.

My saints were often silly men
Fond of wine and loose with women.

When they rose to holy stature
They kept the whims of human nature

Were mystics in their London gardens
Or wore instead of hairshirts burdens

Of a mild domestic sort: but so devout
That suddenly they would go out

And die for freedom in the street
Or fall like partridges before a butt

Of ambush'd tyranny and hate.
Other legends will relate

The tale of men whose only love
Was simple work: whose usual lives

Were formed in mirth and music, or in words

Whose golden echoes are wild rewards

For all our suffering, unto death ...

On the last page a colophon
Would conclude the liberal plan

Showing Man within a frame
Of trophies stolen from a dream.

3

The busy routine kills the flowers
That blossom only on the casual path.
The gift is sacrificed to gain: the gain
Is ploughed into the hungry ground
The best of life is sparely spent
In contemplation of those laws
Illustrious in leaves, in tiny webs
Spun by the ground-spider: in snailshells
And mushroom gills: in acorns and gourds –
The design everywhere evident
The purpose still obscure

                    In a free hour
I walk through the woods with God
When the air is calm and the midges
Hover in the netted sun and stillness.
Deep then I sink in reverie. There is rest
Above the beating heart: the body
Settles round its axis: mind simulates

The crystal in the cooling rock
The theorem in the beetle's eye –
After the day's mutations
Finds the silver node of sleep …

In that peace
Mind looks into a mirror pois'd
Above body: sees in perspective
Guts, bones and glands: the make of a man.
Out of that labyrinth
The man emerges: becomes
What he is: by no grace
Can become other: can only seize
The pattern in the bone, in branching veins
In clever vesicles and valves
And imitate in acts that beauty.

His nature is God's nature: but torn
How torn and fretted by vain energies
The darting images of eye and ear
Veil'd in the web of memory
Drifts of words that deaden
The subtle manuals of sense.
But the pattern once perceiv'd and held
Is then viable; in good gait and going
In fine song and singular sign: in all
God's festival of perfect form.

## 4

Here is my cell: here my houselings
Gentle in love, excelling hate, extending
Tokens of friendship to free hearts.

But well we know there is a world without
Of alarm and horror and extreme distress
Where pity is a bond of fear
And only the still heart has grace.
An ancient road winds through the wood
The wood is dark: a chancel where the mind
Sways in terror of the formal foe.

Their feet upon the peat and sand
Made no sound. But sounds were everywhere around
Life rustled under fallen leaves, rotted twigs
Snapped like rafters above the heads
Of those friars preachers, constant and firm
Who in charity advanced against the Arian hate
Ambush'd against them. See now
The falchion falls: the martyr's limbs
Lie like trimm'd branches on the ground.

    The ancient road winds through the wood
    A path obscure and frail.

    The martyr takes it and the man
    Who makes the martyr by his deed.

    Death waits on evil and on holiness

Death waits in the leafy labyrinth.
There is a grace to still the blood
Of those who take the daring path:
There is a grace that fills the dying eye
With pity for the wielder of the axe.

There is a grace that nulls the pain
Of martyrs in their hour of death.

Death is no pain to desperate men.

Vision itself is desperate: the act
Is born of the ideal: the hand
Must seize the hovering grail.

The sense of glory stirs the heart
Out of its stillness: a white light
Is in the hills and the thin cry
Of a hunter's horn. We shall act
We shall build
A crystal city in the age of peace
Setting out from an island of calm
A limpid source of love.

5

The branches break. The beaters
Are moving in: lie still my loves
Like deer: let the lynx
Glide through the dappled underwoods.
Lie still: he cannot hear: he may not see.

Should the ravening death descend
We will be calm: die like the mouse
Terrified but tender. The claw
Will meet no satisfaction in our sweet flesh
And we shall have known peace

In a house beneath a beechwood
In an acre of wild land.

## A SHORT POEM FOR ARMISTICE DAY

Gather or take fierce degree
trim the lamp set out for sea
here we are at the workmen's entrance
clock in and shed your eminence.

Notwithstanding, work it diverse ways
work it diverse days, multiplying four digestions
here we make artificial flowers
of paper tin and metal thread.

One eye one leg one arm one lung
a syncopated sick heart-beat
the record is not nearly worn
that weaves a background to our work.

I have no power therefore have patience
These flowers have no sweet scent
no lustre in the petal no increase
from fertilising flies and bees.

No seed they have no seed
their tendrils are of wire and grip
the buttonhole the lip
and never fade

And will not fade though life
and lustre go in genuine flowers
and men like flowers are cut
and wither on a stem

And will not fade a year or more
I stuck one in a candlestick
and there it clings about the socket
I have no power therefore have patience.

**1945**

They came running over the perilous sands
    Children with their golden eyes
Crying: *Look! We have found samphire*
    Holding out their bone-ridden hands.

It might have been the spittle of wrens
    Or the silver nest of a squirrel
For I was invested with the darkness
    Of an ancient quarrel whose omens
Lay scatter'd on the silted beach.
    The children came running toward me.

But I saw only the waves behind them
    Cold, salt and disastrous
Lift their black banners and break
    Endlessly, without resurrection.

# *"FREEDOM IS IT A CRIME?"*
# POST-WAR WRITINGS
# ON ANARCHISM AND PACIFISM

# BEFORE THE TRIAL
## from *War Commentary*, 21 April 1945

We are met at a very significant moment in history. We are told that the end of the war in Europe is in sight – a matter of a few days, even of a few hours. The embattled forces of the Allies are closing in from all sides – dancing round the gigantic crater of ruin which is Germany.

Our statesmen have made a chaos and call it victory. Millions of men are dead, and their silence is called peace. Millions of slaves and prisoners stream eastward and westward – to the North and to the South – anywhere from the centre of this ghastly compass of war. As they travel along the dusty roads, they lose their marks of identity, their uniforms and badges – they resume their human shape and appearance: the grey mass of the unemployed. From unemployment they were snatched by the Conscriptors. The war began in Unemployment: the war will end in Unemployment.

A few days ago Eisenhower reported that he had taken two million prisoners since D Day. 'Not enough,' replied Sir James Grigg, 'I want two million *and four.*' At this stage in the unfolding of the European tragedy, four people have been arrested, here in this Land of Liberty. We have met here to ask *Why?*

Why at this final stage of the universal butchery are these four comrades arrested? Is it to be seriously contended that at this twelfth hour any words of theirs could so disaffect members of His Majesty's Forces that the outcome of the war would be in doubt? I hope that that will be the argument, for it would be the biggest compliment ever paid to the philosophy of anarchism. What other charge, in relation to the war – and remember that 39A is a wartime regulation – what other charge is conceivable? I see none, and therefore I conclude that 39A is being used for other than its intended purpose. If I am asked what other purpose is conceivable, I would point to the singular fact that whilst in all other European countries (the so-called neutrals excepted) the fascists or collaborationists have been incautious enough to come out into the open, and have been caught there, *here* they have never emerged from their hiding-places – have never taken off their masks.

There was a time – back in 1940 – when I thought that here too the war would inevitably lead to revolution – that it would be neither won nor lost without a social upheaval. I was wrong. We won the Battle of Britain, but lost the chance of a British Revolution. The fascists – I do not refer to a poor prematurely-born homunculus like Mosley – the fascists kept on their masks, stayed in their hide-outs. There were regulations and controls – lots of them – but the new controller was the old boss writ large. There was no essential change. We were, and in all essentials we have remained, a fascist plutocracy.

Against this crypto-fascism in our midst, only an insignificant minority has hitherto fought openly. Some have fought in a roundabout way – by collaborating with Badoglio in Italy, with King George in Greece, with General de Gaulle in France – I am too naive to appreciate the tactics of our communist friends. But a few people, and prominent among them our four arrested comrades, have fought our home-based fascism openly and directly. They have fought with increasing vigour and growing success. A certain weight of opinion has formed behind them, particularly among members of the younger generation. It seems possible that our fascists in high places have become aware of this small but brilliant band – have seen this small but bright red-light, and have resolved to extinguish it before it becomes a glowing beacon. How else explain a move which on every other interpretation is patently ridiculous?

Comrades, the time for doubts and hesitations is past. Those who waited for the war to bring about a revolution must now repent their mistake. The situation is unequivocal. There will be no revolution – just yet. But from this moment we move into active resistance. The front line of the Resistance Movement is now here, in England, and we, *alone* if necessary, will continue the fight against fascism. We have French comrades, Dutch comrades, Polish comrades, comrades whose underground struggle we have admired. But from now on we must treat them as heroes of another day. We have supported them in their struggle against fascism. We do not now expect them to fraternise with the friends of fascism here. In the moment of their victory we expect them to continue the fight by our side.

That fight will not be conducted in the hills or on the beaches or in any such romantic places – it will be carried into the streets and docks, into slums and factories. Nor shall we fight with block-busters and tanks, not even with tommy-guns and bombs. Our weapons are words, and all we need for success is freedom of speech and expression – 'everywhere in the world'. That is the first of the four freedoms, but what cynical mockery is this which in the moment of victory falls on our comrades on no other charge than the exercise of that freedom. But we shall not suffer their persecution. We do not challenge any law that is natural, any trial that is just. But we stand firm in asserting the traditional rights which free men in this country have fought for throughout the centuries and we challenge that State which, with arbitrary authority and ignoble instruments – I refer to our political police – has dared to abrogate those traditional rights: we challenge that State to an unrelenting strife. It is a small group of anarchists whose freedom is threatened, but, comrades, I do not speak to you now as an anarchist: I speak to you as an Englishman, as one proud to follow in the tradition of Milton and Shelley – the tradition of all those poets and philosophers who have given us the proud right to claim freedom of speech and the liberty of unlicensed printing. For that, comrades, is the issue, and in that issue we shall engage our personal liberty and if necessary our lives.

We could give our comrades many inspiring words to remember as they stand in the dock next week, but most of all I would like them to remember those words which an American Quaker addressed to an American jury during the last war, when he was facing a similar charge. That Quaker's name was Eugene V. Debs, and here are the beautiful words he used on that occasion:

'Gentlemen of the Jury, I am accused of having obstructed the war. I admit it. Gentlemen, I abhor war. I would oppose the war if I stood alone. I believe that nations have been pitted against nations long enough in hatred ...

'I am opposed to war. I am perfectly willing on that account to be branded as a traitor. And if it is a crime under the American law to be opposed to human bloodshed, I am perfectly willing to be branded as a criminal and to end my days in a prison cell ...

'And now, Gentlemen of the Jury, I am prepared for the sentence. I will accept your verdict. What you will do to me does not matter much. Years ago I recognised my kinship with all living beings, and I made up my mind that I was not one whit better than the meanest of earth. I said then, and I say now, that while there is a lower class I am in it: while there is a criminal element I am of it: while there is a soul in prison, I am not free.'

Like Eugene Debs, our four comrades have dared to stand firm in the cause of humanity. What they have said, all lovers of peace and freedom have said and will continue to say. Our comrades go to trial as our representatives. In the hour of their trial, and after their trial, whatever its outcome, we shall not fail them. If the four are imprisoned, forty will step into the breach and carry on. If forty are imprisoned four hundred will be there to take their place. We have been challenged: we accept the challenge. We will fight: fight the Defence Regulations and that foul and un-English institution, the political police. We will fight tyranny and oppression in every shape and form, everywhere in the world, until freedom is finally a reality, and justice a natural right.

# AFTER THE TRIAL
from Herbert Read's *Freedom: Is it a Crime?*
(London: Freedom Press, 1945)

At our last meeting I said that if our comrades were imprisoned, we who remained free would continue the struggle against the forces of repression now active in this country, against the political police, against every enemy of freedom. That struggle is now on. The weapons with which we can fight are limited: they are the very weapons which our authoritarian government is attempting to take away from us – our printing press, our pamphlets, our right to speak and publish the truth that is within us. Limited as they are, these are nevertheless the only weapons we need to create such a volume of protest that press and parliament, the public at large will be compelled to listen to us. We shall not rest until our comrades are released, and even then we shall go on, to create such a consciousness of the existing danger to our common liberty, that the cause of it is for ever eliminated from our society.

It will not be an easy campaign. Among the many lessons which this episode has taught us, the most surprising to me has been the indifference of the so-called liberal press. There have been exceptions, and in particular I would like to mention the *Manchester Guardian*. But for the most part, once they had exhausted the 'news value' of the case in a sentence or two, the rest has been silence. Here was a clear threat to the liberty of the Press. Did the Press rise in righteous indignation? We have not heard a single note of complaint. This institution which boasts that it is the guardian of our national liberties was perhaps a little drunk with the prospects of a military victory: at any rate, it slept whilst the very liberties which they thought were being secured in Europe, were filched from us here in the Old Bailey.

Then there is Parliament. We anarchists have never placed much faith in the dim inmates of that opium den, but we note that many of them talk frequently of liberty, inside the House and out. But what has Parliament done to defend our liberty in this case? We know well enough that all that gang talk endlessly about freedom, it is a nice inspiring word – but they uphold its reality only so long as it does not threaten their private interests.

In these last few weeks more hypocrisy has been smeared over our daily and weekly papers than ever before in our history. If you can bring yourself to read the leading articles and commentaries in these periodicals, you will find the word 'freedom' in almost every paragraph. You are told that we have just won the greatest war in history – for 'freedom'. You are asked to celebrate this glorious victory 'in the cause of freedom.' You are even encouraged to get drunk for 'freedom.' We are not deceived. So long as our three comrades remain in prison, victory is an illusion, and the man who celebrates it is nothing but a mug.

We have met here tonight not to celebrate a victory, but to take counsel after a defeat. In the face of that defeat, I propose now briefly to reaffirm the beliefs for which our comrades have been persecuted and imprisoned. It would give me great pleasure to do this if only to show that we are by no means intimidated by what has happened. The penalties of the Courts are only justified on the assumption that they deter others from repeating the alleged offence. We are not moved one inch from our course. All that legal pantomime at the Old Bailey was from every point of view a futile and costly farce. It has cost our side quite a lot: it must have cost the State more – several thousand pounds. There are the salaries of Inspector Whitehead and his agents for the three or four months they devoted to the case: there are the still larger salaries of the Attorney General and his assistants for the many days they devoted to the reading of *War Commentary*: the still larger salary of his lordship the Judge for the four days he spent listening to the case: and then the more modest wages of the ushers who tried to keep us out of the Court and of all the various clerks and bailiffs who filled the benches in the Court. Nor must we forget the wages of the policemen who inspected all our identity cards one day. That makes a pretty total which might have been justified if the prisoners on trial had been gangsters or profiteers, murderers or swindlers.

But what in actual fact were the prisoners in the dock? They were men who held a certain belief, a theory of society, an ideal of civilisation, and all they had done, the only crime with which they could be charged, was that they had incidentally taken steps to bring their beliefs to the attention of members of His Majesty's Forces.

What is this belief whose mere propagation constitutes a crime? I am going to tell you, in simple direct words, and what I shall say will amount to no more and no less than the substance of the beliefs for which our comrades are now suffering a sentence of imprisonment.

We begin with the central fact of WAR. We say that if our civilisation is to survive – not this country nor that country, but the whole civilisation of which we are members – war must be eliminated. War has now reached a stage of technical development which in future will involve, not merely the deaths of millions of human beings – men, women and children – but also the complete destruction of material necessities of life: food, housing, communications, health. War will henceforth mean annihilation, not merely for the vanquished, but for all who engage in it.

We then analyse the causes of war, and this is where we begin to differ from other people who would also like to get rid of war. We say that modern war cannot be explained in terms of capitalism, of imperialism, of economics or of populations: it is a disease of civilisation itself, something inherent in the very structure of modern society. In order to get rid of war, we must alter the structure of society.

But 'to alter the structure of society' is merely a polite way of saying that a revolution will be essential, and it is for using this word 'revolution' that our comrades are in prison. They would not have been put in prison if they had expressed a wish to alter 'the structure of society' – which only shows what power is attributed to *words* when they become *weapons*.

But whatever we call the process, the choice before our civilisation is clear: either revolution or annihilation. That is the unescapable conclusion which we anarchists have reached, and we claim that it is a rational, indeed a logical conclusion.

But what then does revolution imply? We say that the structural fault in our civilisation which leads to war lies in the doctrine of national sovereignty, which requires for its expression and propagation the social organ known as the State. Modern wars are conducted by States, through their paid servants – the politicians, civil servants and armed forces.

Wars do not, in our stage of development, break out naturally between *peoples*, and in spite of all the powers of persuasion which States can command and direct, the peoples remain largely indifferent to the issues involved in State wars. Put in another way, we might say that modern wars are essentially ideological, and ideologies belong to classes, not to peoples. The peoples have no ideologies anywhere. They have interests and prejudices, customs and superstitions: they may be selfish and egotistic, but everywhere and at all time their main purpose is to secure a living from the soil, or from the labours of their hands or brains: and they know that such a purpose is not furthered, but frustrated, by war. Lives, houses, cattle, tillage, material possessions of every kind – these are the common wealth of the people, however unevenly distributed that wealth may be. That kind of wealth is destroyed by war. What is not destroyed by war is another kind of wealth – gold, bonds, credits and other goods not made by labour: these may escape war, just as German Bonds will survive this war, or as Russian Imperial Bonds have escaped 'the greatest revolution in history': but this kind of wealth does not belong to the people, but to the State and its servants, and, one must add, to its dupes.

Under defeat, a particular State may disintegrate. We have seen several States disintegrate during the past few years – France, Belgium, Italy, Greece, and now Germany. This, we say, provides a golden opportunity to make the necessary structural alterations in our social system. It is, in fact, a revolutionary situation, and in such a situation, when the State has revealed all its insubstantiality, and has vanished overnight, we must not let any body of gangsters or looters step out of the ruins and organise another State. That will only lead inevitably to another war and a worse war. In such a revolutionary situation, our comrades said, and I repeat, the armed forces have ceased to exist as instruments of a State: for the moment the nations have become peoples, people in arms. Let the nation remain a people in arms – stick to your arms, we say to such a people, rather than deliver them up to any gang which takes on itself to speak in the name of a new State. If we are a people, all equal and all equally armed or disarmed, then we can get together and agree on a new form of society, a non-governmental society, in which nation will no longer be opposed to nation, State to State, but a society in which people will work together for the common good. When that reform has been accomplished, everywhere in the world, we can all throw away our arms, and live in peace ever after.

That is the doctrine which our comrades preached, for which they have been persecuted and imprisoned. You may not agree with it – you may not agree with Buddhism or Christianity, with communism or conservatism, but we do not, in this country, imprison people for being Buddhists or Christians, conservatives or communists. Why, then, in the name of all that is just and equitable, are these three anarchists deprived of their liberty?

Well, it is perhaps a simple miscarriage of justice, an anomaly of the law, some bad kind of joke played by the State jesters. That would be the most agreeable explanation to offer. But if that is not the right explanation, if our comrades have been imprisoned in the pursuance of a ruthless and determined policy, then the rights we believe we possess as citizens of this democratic country are at an end. There is no longer in this land such a thing as the liberty of unlicensed printing for which Milton made his immortal and unanswerable plea: there is no longer any such thing as freedom of expression which ten generations of Englishmen have jealously guarded. These words are now a mockery, and either we have been duped slaves to accept such a breach of our traditional rights, or we resolve never to rest until they are restored. I cannot imagine what perfidy of mind has spread among our judiciary that it has so far forgotten its trust as to allow so great an abuse of justice under the excuse of wartime regulations – regulations which peace has now made obsolete. Some of these Regulations have just been abolished – the fascists have been set free, but our comrades remain in prison. These Regulations which were admitted under protest at the time of their enactment, and only accepted in view of their temporary force, were designed, however illogically, to secure a victory in the cause of freedom. By all accounts, that victory has been won. But we are here to assert that the war which has been won on the Continent of Europe has been lost in this island of Britain, and we can have no joy in victory, nor ease from strife, until our comrades once more stand beside us as free men.

# AMNESTY CAMPAIGN
## from *Freedom*, 25 August 1945

*We reproduce below a statement which has been issued to the press by the Freedom Defence Committee in connection with their campaign for an amnesty for people held in British prisons under wartime regulations and laws. The campaign was initiated by the display of posters calling upon the people to demand such an amnesty, and we reproduce the photograph of these posters. Already there have been many signatures to the demand for an amnesty and the activities of the committee have received the support of many people, of various opinions, who realise the danger at the present time of the complete loss of our elementary civil liberties unless some really vigorous body exists for resisting the progress of reaction and regimentation, even when it appears under the guise of Labour government.*

*The Committee intends shortly to start a second campaign against the continuance of military and industrial conscription.*

Although the war in Europe has ended, and the fascist internees have been released from their confinement, thousands of men and women are still in prison under wartime laws. These prisoners are not offenders against the common law, and the regulations under which they were incarcerated are admitted to be extraordinary measures necessitated only by the emergency of a major war.

They include political prisoners (whom the law chooses to class as felons), conscientious objectors, deserters, absentees and offenders under many bureaucratic regulations. The civil prisons are overcrowded with them, and many more are held under appalling conditions in military concentration camps, often undergoing long sentences for trifling offences.

Whatever excuse may have been given during the past few years for such imprisonments is surely invalidated now that the war in Europe is ended and we are told that the nation will gradually return to peacetime conditions. The most important task of a return to peace, more urgent even than housing or food, would appear to be a rectification of those injustices which were committed during wartime when the fundamental rights of the citizen were suspended under the pretext of an emergency situation. It is to be hoped that the new Labour government will take early action to alter this situation.

The Freedom Defence Committee intends to begin an immediate campaign for an amnesty for all civilian and military offenders against wartime laws, and would welcome the support of all who are anxious for the liberation of the British prisoners of war in British prisons. A demand for such an amnesty will be presented to the Home Secretary, and signature forms are available from the offices of the Committee, 17 St George Street, Hanover Square, London W1.

The Freedom Defence Committee was originated in February of this year under the name of the Freedom Press Defence Committee, to assist the four anarchists who were being tried under Regulation 39A. At that time it became evident that there was a need for a permanent vigilance body to fight for the preservation of elementary civil liberties, and the Freedom Defence Committee, consisting of individuals of many different shades of liberal, socialist and libertarian opinion, was formed for that purpose.

**Herbert Read, Chairman**
**Freedom Defence Committee**

# THE PROBLEM OF WAR AND PEACE
from *Freedom*, 20 September 1947

*Science, Liberty and Peace* by Aldous Huxley and *War, Sadism and Pacifism* by Edward Glover. This piece was originally a radio broadcast on the BBC Home Service.

THE fear of war continues to be the pre-occupation of the whole world, and a great deal of our time and money is spent, either on efforts to establish and preserve peace, or on preparations for still another war. But do we really understand the nature of the problem of war and peace? How is it conceivable that we, who are gifted with rational faculties, and are citizens of a common world, will presently proceed to destroy each other with the terrible weapons which modern science has put in our hands, and for reasons which are merely economic, or political, or ideological. We all know that the atomic warfare of the future will exceed even the last war in horror, terror, and the destruction of life and civilization. Why, then do we not merely contemplate the possibility of such a war, but even despairingly admit its inevitability? Why cannot mankind be sane when its very existence is threatened by causes which *should* be within the control of reason, of science, of pity?

The two authors whose books we are considering have different answers to these questions. Mr Huxley, in spite of the mysticism which to an increasing extent dominates his writings, is really an optimistic rationalist. The 'Inner Light' does, it is true, make its fitful appearance in this new tract for the times. He says that if only 'ministers of the various sects and religions would abandon sentimentality and superstition, and devote themselves to teaching their flocks that the Final End of man is not in the unknowable Utopian future, but in the timeless eternity of the Inner Light, which every human begin is capable, if he so desires, of realising here and now, then the myth of progress would lose its harmfulness as a justifier of present tyranny and wrongdoing.' But, alas, sighs Mr Huxley, the average human being will never attain this timeless eternity of Inner Light because he is fascinated by a will o' wisp which he calls science, and which, far from leading him to Utopia, is creating round him a social and economic hell of which war, in all its scientific efficiency, is merely one aspect.

Mr Huxley's pamphlet is really a frontal attack on the amoral scientific mind of today. It is the scientist who, without any sense of moral values, and overriding conception of goodness or beauty, has created social tendencies which inevitably lead to the concentration of power in irresponsible hands, to a centralisation of industry in amorphous inhuman cities, to a world-wide condition of economic insecurity which can only be resolved by war. The ideals of science are always in the direction of more and more power, more and more production, greater speed and completer mechanisation, and along with these materialistic ideals goes a mental attitude which accepts such quantitative achievements as progress, and believes that such progress is the only object in life.

No one, I think, can question this diagnosis of the materialistic trends of our civilisation, nor deny their connection with man's insane proneness to war. But what we must question is the assumption which Mr Huxley then makes, that we have only to redirect these scientific trends in order to secure peace. 'Let us suppose,' he says, 'that those who make it their business to apply the results of pure science to economic ends should elect to do so, not primarily for the benefit of big business, big cities and big government, but with the conscious aim of providing individuals with the means of doing profitable and intrinsically significant work, of helping men and women to achieve independence from bosses, so that they may become their own employers, or members of a self-governing, co-operative group working for subsistence and a local market.' Suppose, repeats Mr Huxley, 'that this were henceforward to become the acknowledged purpose guiding the labours of inventors and engineers.' Why, then, cries Mr Huxley, a progressive decentralisation of population, of ownership of the means of production, of political and economic power, would become possible. We could increase the local sources of food supply by improving insect controls and multiplying refrigerator units; we could develop entirely new foods such as edible yeasts; we could synthetise chlorophyll; and as for fuel (which as present causes so much international tension) we could revive windmills and construct paraboloid mirrors of large size which would be capable of superheating steam and even of melting iron by direct action of the sun's rays.

O brave new world! But Mr Huxley does not tell us how the chemist and the biologist, the physicist and the engineer are to be persuaded to see the Inner Light, and redirect their energies towards such eminently reasonable ends as decentralisation and regional co-operation.

A change of heart such as Mr Huxley requires is a psychological process, so let us turn to Dr Glover, one of the leading psychoanalysts in this country. He has just published a new edition of a book he wrote fourteen years ago, but the new volume is more than twice the size of the old one, and its argument has been greatly strengthened by the material evidence provided by another world war. If I say that I regard this book as the most important contribution ever made to the solution of the problem of war and peace, I shall be accused of exaggeration and defeat my aim, which is to persuade you to read *War, Sadism and Pacifism*. But what, in the whole range of science and politics, could be more important than a solution of this problem? If a scientist has put his finger on the real cause of war, and has indicated methods by means of which war might be prevented, then not even the invention of anaesthetics or antiseptics, the cure of cancer or tuberculosis, could claim to be more important. Diseases ravage our lives, but war destroys civilisation itself, and all that makes life worth living. So please listen to what Dr Glover has to say.

Dr Glover is a scientist and he is using scientific language which cannot wholly, or accurately, be translated into the language of everyday life. But I shall try to restate his thesis in simple words. He begins with the fact that we are all creatures compounded of love and hate. We are born into a world of harsh reality, and from the very first days of our lives we have to struggle against forces which threaten our inborn selfish instincts. We have to fight for food, for air, for freedom of movement, and in that struggle we turn against the very objects of our love – our mothers, our fathers, our brothers and sisters. But for one reason or another we do not, or we cannot, express this hatred: we are *frustrated* and therefore bury or *repress* those unsocial, disloyal, ungrateful feelings. We are then no longer conscious of their existence, but psychoanalysis has proved beyond any doubt that such feelings continue to exist, in a deep and inaccessible region of the mind: that they are bottled up, as it were, under pressure, and continually seek objects upon which they can vent their hateful force.

Opportunities for such a discharge of hatred do not normally occur in the orderly conventional life we lead in peacetime, so the energy accumulates until we find an excuse for war, and there occurs a catastrophic purgation of our overcharged emotional system.

What we have to do, in order to prevent war, is to make sure that our aggressive instincts are not frustrated and repressed, especially during the period of infancy. We cannot get rid of the primary instincts of hatred – they are part of our human heritage, the curse with which we are all born. But we can hope to reduce the mental strains which cause outbreaks of irrational violence, delinquency, crime and war. 'Reduce unconscious anxieties,' says Dr Glover, 'and hostile reactions begin to disappear.' In the individual this can be done by a short-term policy of psychoanalysis and mental therapy or healing. But you cannot, in this way, treat all the millions of individuals that constitute the warring nations. So a long-term policy of social analysis and social therapy is needed. That policy, to be effective, must be carried out in the formative stages of the disease: it is a preventive therapy, or prophylactic, and it must take place in the nursery, in the home, in the school. 'I do not believe,' says Dr Glover, 'that war between civilised nations will ever be prevented until we learn how to bring up children in a more reasonable and understanding way than we do at present.' But a more reasonable and understanding way implies measures which will shock the conventional citizen and parent. For – it is no use disguising the fact – our impulses of hatred are closely related to our sexual impulses, and one of the first things we must do is to try and reduce what Dr Glover calls 'the tangled mass of superstitions and conventions that obstruct all rational adaptation to sexual life.' 'It is difficult,' he says, 'to overestimate the reduction in emotional friction that could be secured if more rational codes were applied to sexual problems from infancy onwards.' But the essence of any such reform is that it should be carried out in an atmosphere of love and intimacy. 'The really shocking thing about Western Civilization,' Dr Glover thinks, 'is that it permits and approves, on both cultural and economic grounds, the delegation of upbringing from the family to every conceivable form of substitute parent or training institution. To my mind it is much more shocking that Anglo-Indian parents should board out their little three or four years old children in Bognor than that a native mother should go to work with her baby slung over her back, or that little tribal children should carry on their sexual play before the indulgent and amused eyes of their parents. Indeed, I would go so far as to say that the successful upbringing of children requires a Renaissance of Family Culture. The family must somehow or other win back from the State the rights it has lost; and it must re-establish a scale of values in which the place of honour is given, not to social achievement, but to transmission of humane family culture.'

There is no time to enter into any further detail of the diagnosis which Dr Glover makes, or of the preventive measures which he prescribes. Many of his practical recommendations are the same as Mr Huxley's – he agrees, for example, that the centralisation of power and production and the worship of the State are the symptoms of our social neurosis: that the main problem is 'how to extend the cultural authority assumed by the family and to curtail the spurious cultural authority assumed by the State.' But he knows that we cannot rely on anything so uncertain as a change of heart. He believes that the problem is a scientific one, but he fears that unless scientists know how to manipulate the forces of love and hate they will make a greater mess of government than any laymen. For our politicians he has nothing but contempt: 'undaunted by an endless and humiliating story of absolute failure, they continue their labours with unruffled faith in the rule of thumb.' Some entirely new method of approach to the problem is essential, and that method is suggested by the theory and practice of psychoanalysis.

On the basis of that theory and practice we can at least be sure that 'any investigation of the subject which neglects to correlate war phenomena with primitive infantile phases of unconscious mental development can only end in futility and frustration' – a difficult sentence which means that the war to end war must be fought long before our children reach the playing-fields of Eton or of any other school.

We need a new science of upbringing, and for a few of the millions now spent on UNO, UNESCO and the armaments of a fear-ridden world, we could have it.

# A ONE-MAN MANIFESTO
## from *Freedom*, 3 March 1951

THE most terrifying object in the world today is not the atom bomb but the political cliché. The political cliché is not merely verbal: the words reflect a mental reaction which is as automatic as it is false. It projects its own guilt feelings onto a chosen object – it used to be a harmless animal object, the scapegoat, but now it has to be a human object, the enemy, to whom we give a dehumanised name: the boche, the nazi, the red. Human guilt is now so enormous, that millions of scapegoats are needed to carry it. The human race is accordingly divided into two moieties, each serving as the scapegoat of the other.

To listen to the purveyors of clichés, the so-called statesmen, the politicians, generals and journalists, has become an inescapable infliction. Not to know the news is now a crime: ignorance is connivance and innocence is guilt. In a spirit of scientific detachment it becomes almost fascinating to watch this automatic projection of clichés: Dulles, Truman, Taft, Attlee, Bevin, Eden, Schuman and Adenauer – they are all the same. If by chance a public figure gets up and makes an utterance that is not a cliché – as Pastor Niemoller has been doing lately – there is a shocked surprise, as if an indecency has been committed in public. But that is a very rare occurrence.

The present alarm is not difficult to understand. Since the end of the last war (indeed since the end of the First World War) the spread of a phenomenon to which we give the name 'communism' has been continuous. It suffers from apparent set-backs (Yugoslavia), but these are not of a nature to give any real satisfaction to the opponents of communism. Communism now embraces about half the world and the more widely diffused it becomes, the less easy it is to define. The conversion of the four hundred millions of China to communism is not an ideological phenomenon: it is in the nature of a mental landslide. Millions wake up one morning and find that they are communists. Theirs is not to reason why: life goes on as before, with perhaps a change of landlords to mark the event; and, of course, a different symbol on the flag and a call-up to a people's army. But in the army it is the same drill, just as in the fields it is the same relentless toil.

The people who get excited (Dr Comfort's delinquents) are the people who run the bulldozers that cause the political landslides. These bulldozers are very powerful machines, serviced by fanatical politicians and journalists, and they go about the world bulldozing over peasants and workers and in a general way creating chaos – shovelling millions into the armament factories, millions into the armed forces, and millions more into the 'lines of communication'. No one is allowed to get on with his natural function, which may be producing food, or building houses, or writing poetry.

The odd thing is that we all submit to this bulldozing. Hardly a squeak is to be heard. We are pushed here and we are pushed there, and at the end of the week we hand over up to half our pay in taxes to feed the bulldozers, to keep them going against us. Nothing is so significant of the present age, and perhaps a symptom of its incurable decadence, as the prevailing apathy in all countries – the refusal to fight the bulldozing politicians and generals, *the willingness to pay*. It was not always so. Our liberties were won by the simple expedient of refusing to furnish the means (ship-money, etc) of bulldozing the people. Such a practical procedure is not even discussed these days. Technically it may be treason: but it was by 'treason' that we won the Magna Carta and every other advance in political liberty.

Most significant in this muted slaughterhouse we live in is the apathy and inefficiency of the Christian churches and of the secular pacifist movements. Though the churches profess, in accordance with the teachings of Christ, a belief in peace, they take no effective steps to instil that belief in their congregations (Pastor Niemoller and his following excepted). They merely bless the rival combatants.

As for the breakdown of secular pacifism, it seems to be pathological. A belief requiring the highest degree of moral courage and personal sacrifice, there are no more than a handful of men in any country who are ready to propagate this belief, and they are mostly of an older generation. The youth in all countries is indifferent to pacifist propaganda and accepts with fatalistic indifference the militaristic evils which they have inherited.

So much for the general diagnosis. Immediately, at the opening of the year 1951, there is the danger, indeed already the actuality, of a Third World War. The communist revolution in China, completely successful, has thrown the United States into a truculent panic. In defiance of all political decorum or absolute justice, this powerful nation clings desperately to a discredited régime lodged precariously in the Chinese island of Formosa. On the mainland, with the support of the democratic half-world, she has invaded Korea on a pretext of broken treaties. China has now retaliated and threatens to drive the invaders across the sea. The United States call for a wider war, a war that cannot be restricted to China, but must inevitably involve Western Europe and virtually the whole world.

It is at this point that the complete unreality of the situation becomes evident. The United States has a cover in the United Nations, an organisation dedicated to high ideals of a democratic character. Such ideals are supposedly an expression of the will of the people, and they do indeed represent the popular desire for peace. It is difficult to say *who wants war*. Certainly not the people – not the people in any country in the world. Certain politicians, perhaps; certain military commanders, perhaps; some calculating financiers ad manufacturers. But it is difficult to believe, in the pre-war fashion, that a few scheming politicians, generals and capitalists are capable nowadays, for their private benefit, and against the will of the people, of precipitating a world war twice in a generation. Preparations for war keep certain industries at full stretch, but we have discovered that there is no certain profit, material or moral, for anybody in modern war. We can only conclude with a psychologist like Jung, that unconscious motives of a collectivist nature are responsible for such mass insanity.

If that is the case, there are only two possibilities – either to acquiesce in the drift to world destruction, on the assumption that individual action is futile; or to enter upon a course of action which would in effect be a mass self-analysis, leading to the exposure of unconscious motives. What form such analysis should take is more than I can say, though I have made suggestions in *Education for Peace*. But no analysis or cure can take place unless the patient has the will to be cured. There is no sign of such a will anywhere among the peoples of the world. How should we recognise such signs? The first would be an absence of fear. Fear inhibits the cure of sick minds. In our half-world we fear the unknown, perhaps in the shape of communism, perhaps in no shape at all.

Why are we afraid of communism (in its Russian shape)? Fundamentally because we are afraid of insecurity, of any change in our standards of living. But those standards of living are changing all the time, and insecurity already exists. It is war, and the immense economic burdens due to war, that have created insecurity in our minds and inflation and uncertainty in our economic affairs. It is doubtful if any of the political and economic rigours of a communistic state *without* the burdens of war, could be worse than our so-called democratic way of life *with* the burdens of war. This is to leave out of account the non-material aspects of communism ('freedom'), but to that problem I will come presently.

Our fear of communism is fundamentally a distrust of our own social and economic order – it is the sick man's fear of vitality in others. We do not believe passionately, mystically or even rationally, in whatever social and economic order prevails in our half-world today, for the truth is that no order of any positive kind does exist. There are only various degrees of disorder – of private capitalism in decay, of monopoly capitalism at war with labour monopolies, of state capitalism the prey of apathy and absenteeism. There is no healthy society anywhere in the world today, unless (which I doubt) in Russia.

The way to lose fear, and incidentally to oppose the communism of the Soviet half-world, is to create an integrated social order in our half-world – an order that would challenge the Soviet order, not in military terms, but in social amenities and cultural achievements.

This cannot be done without a revolutionary desire to create such an order throughout our half-world; and there can be no question of creating such an order in a war atmosphere and with an economy dedicated to the provision of armaments.

Immediate unilateral disarmament is the necessary preliminary to the creation of such an order. The decision to disarm would in itself be an act of moral strength sufficing for a further advance to a new world. But such a decision can only be made as an act of faith – an act of faith in humanity.

With such a faith we could resist communism in the only sense which it can be effectively resisted – by conversion. Even if we had to go through a stage of Soviet domination of the world, the passive fortitude of our humanism would in the end triumph over the active evil of inhumanism. That is the minimum faith on which a rational view of life can be based. All this can be easily dismissed as vague idealism, but there is no alternative belief – only as alternatives a nihilistic despair or a destructive spirit of aggression that must overwhelm the whole world.

# DISOBEDIENCE
## from *Peace News*, 20 January 1961

The case for civil disobedience is the case of the individual conscience against the authority of the government. So long as government is absolute and tyrannical there are few reasonable people who would not admit the right of the individual to revolt when his conscience is outraged by a power that has no respect for humanity.

The problem becomes more difficult when the government is a democratic one, and claims to respect the will of the people. But even democratic governments represent only a majority of the people, and sometimes (as in our own country) by a very small margin.

The case for civil disobedience in a democratic society is not so obvious as it is in a tyrannical state, but modern democracy is a very impure institution. Its authority rests on an election in which many diverse and inconsistent policies are presented to the public, and any one vote may be determined by any one of a hundred issues. There has never been a vote on the unequivocal issue of peace or war, and certainly never a vote on whether our country should commit itself to the manufacture and use of atomic weapons

But even if there had been such a vote and the majority was in favour of such a policy, I should still be prepared to disobey the authority of a government that proposed to use such weapons against our fellow men.

I believe there are convincing strategical and political arguments for nuclear disarmament, but I will not use them on this occasion. They are known to most of you and have been

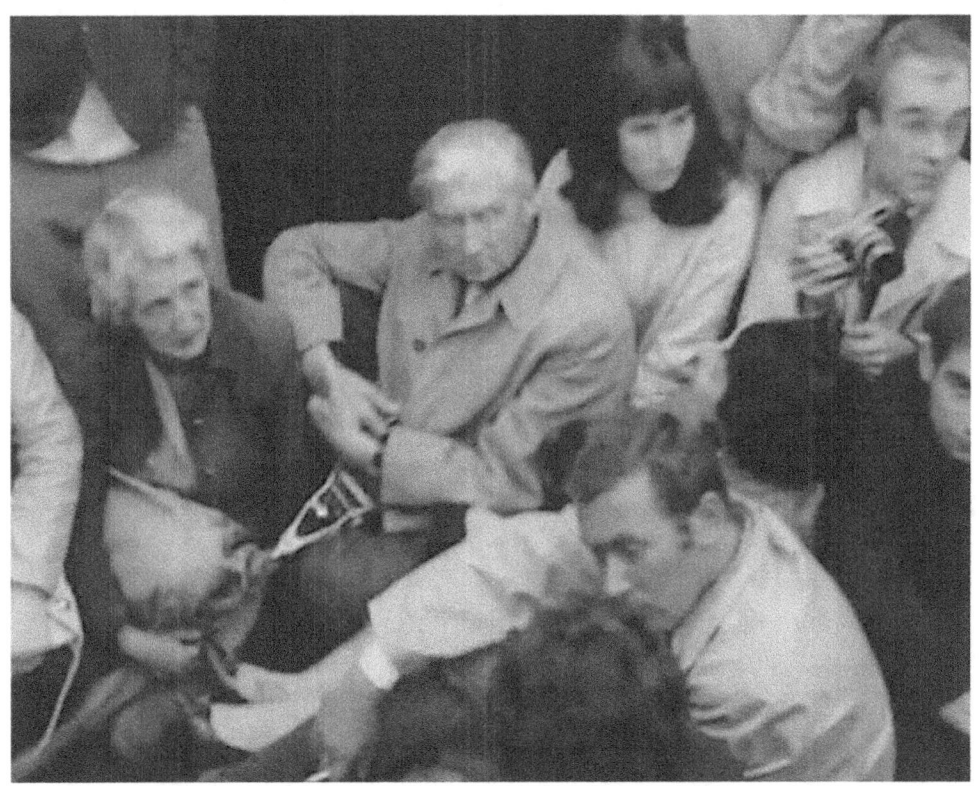

Herbert Read with John Osborne, Sophie Read and others in a sit-down protest at the 'Ban the Bomb' march, Trafalgar Square, London, 1961

expounded with more political acumen than I can claim to possess. My intention to commit an act of civil disobedience in opposition to an official policy that contemplates atomic warfare is neither strategical nor political: it is instinctive.

War itself is instinctive: its immediate causes are economic, but governments would not be able to delude their people into aggressive and murderous acts. But there are certain frustrations common to all of us - emotional tensions caused in us by social conventions that are basically an aspect of the struggle for survival. Frustration automatically arouses aggressive impulses - this is one of the most established of all psychological laws.

To survive without war the society of nations must so arrange its economy and morals that frustration is not entailed with mutual danger to its constituent members, but that is a long-term policy for statesmen, and meanwhile the stockpile of atomic weapons increases. Stupid and bewildered men rise to power and the whole fate of humanity is attached to a very delicate trigger.

To have reached this state of imminent peril is in itself an unparalleled disaster for which the statesmen and scientists of the world have forfeited all moral authority. Not one of us has any longer any faith in political action. The more conferences and committees we arrange and attend the farther away we seem to get from any immediate and practical intention to disarm.

This stalemate must be broken, but it will never be broken by rational argument. There are too many right reasons for the wrong actions on both sides. It can be broken only by instinctive action. An act of disobedience is instinctive: civil disobedience should be collectively instinctive - a revolt of the instincts of man against the threat of mass destruction.

Instincts are dangerous things to play with, but that is why, in the presence of a desperate situation, we must play with instincts. The apathetic indifference of the majority of people to the very real threat of universal destruction is partly due to a lack of imagination, but the imagination does not function in the present situation because it is paralysed by fear in its subconscious sources.

We must release the imagination of the people so that they become fully conscious of the fate that is threatening them, and we can best reach their imagination by our actions, by our fearlessness, by our willingness to sacrifice our comfort, our liberty, and even our lives to the end that mankind shall be delivered from pain and suffering and universal death.

# DECLARATION
## Sent to the Ministry of Defence, London, 1 March 1961
### (recorded in *Hansard*, HC Deb 01 March 1961 vol. 635 c134W)

The nuclear powers of East and West are holding the people of the world to ransom. It is time for the people to act.

Today we are taking positive action against the insane nuclear policies of our Government. We demand the immediate scrapping of the agreement to base Polaris carrying submarines in Britain. We demand the complete rejection by our country of nuclear weapons and all policies and alliances that depend upon them.

Hitler tried to wipe out a whole people. Today the nuclear tyrants of East and West threaten the entire human race with extinction.

We call upon people everywhere to rise up against this monstrous tyranny. We call upon the scientists to refuse to work on nuclear weapons. We call upon workers to "black" all work connected with them and use their industrial strength in the struggle for life. We call upon people from all walks of life to take direct action to bring the production of nuclear weapons to a halt.

Our action this day is the first step in a campaign of non-violent civil disobedience. We hereby serve notice on our Government that we can no longer stand aside while they prepare to destroy mankind.

Augustus John, Herbert Read,
Bertrand Russell and Michael Scott

Running? Oh well!
The mile in sixteen
seven eighths, or
something like that.

*Also available from*
*The Orage Press*

## Between the Riccall and the Rye
**by Herbert Read**
**Edited by Michael Paraskos and Benedict Read**

In this collection of writings we hear Read tell in a straightforward but moving way his memories of a Yorkshire childhood. Through his poetry and prose we gain a real sense of his longing to return to the Yorkshire into which he was born, and once he does return in later life, his profound sense of belonging to this landscape.

**ISBN: 978-09565-802-1-4**

---

## Alfred Orage and the Leeds Arts Club (1893-1923)
**by Tom Steele**

When first published in 1990 Tom Steele's pioneering study into the Leeds Arts Club revolutionized the assumptions underpinning the study of British modernism. Far from being a London-centred affair, radical modernist thinking had a profound impact on regional centres such as Leeds, out of which key figures in the development of world modernism, including Herbert Read, emerged.

**ISBN: 978-09544-523-8-4**

www.ingramcontent.com/pod-product-compliance
Lightning Source LLC
Chambersburg PA
CBHW081839230426
43669CB00018B/2758